CONTEMPORAR

BOOK FIVE
1975 TO 1992

Developed by Contemporary Books, Inc., and General Learning Corporation, Northbrook, Illinois

Copyright © 1992 by Contemporary Books, Inc.
All rights reserved

Published by Contemporary Books, Inc.
Two Prudential Plaza, Chicago, Illinois 60601-6790
Manufactured in the United States of America
International Standard Book Number: 0-8092-4015-7

Library of Congress Cataloging-in-Publication Data

(Revised for volume 5)

Amazing century.

    p.   cm.
   Includes indexes.
   Contents: bk. 1. 1900–1929 — bk. 2. 1929–1945 — (etc.) — bk. 5. 1975 to 1992.
   1. Civilization, Modern—20th century.   2. United States—Civilization—20th century.   I. Contemporary Books, inc.
E169.1.A47186   1992   973.9   91-35292
ISBN 0-8092-4020-3 (pbk. : bk. 1)
ISBN 0-8092-4018-1 (pbk. : bk. 2)
ISBN 0-8092-4017-3 (pbk. : bk. 3)

Editorial Director
Caren Van Slyke

Assistant Editorial Director
Mark Boone

Project Editor
Sarah Conroy

Editorial
Christine M. Benton
Pat Fiene

Editorial Production Manager
Norma Fioretti

Production Editor
Marina Micari

Cover Design
Georgene Sainati

Cover Photo
Niedenthal/Time

Executive Editor
Laura Ruekberg

Managing Editor
Alan Lenhoff

Associate Editor
Miriam Greenblatt

Assistant Editor
David Bristow

Art Director
Ami Koenig

Research
Sam Johnson
Therese Shinners
Betty Tsamis

To Our Readers

The collapse of communism in the Soviet Union and Eastern Europe . . . the hostage crisis in Iran . . . the tragedy of the Challenger *explosion . . . the disco craze . . . the rap revolution . . . the frightening AIDS epidemic . . .*

In the pages of this book are some of the biggest news stories of our day. The photographs and stories in this book reach out to us. They tell about people and events that have helped to shape this century—and make our nation what it is today.

Though you may not know all the faces and places, you'll recognize many of the stories behind them. You'll see that today's news stories have their roots in the past—and that we have many things in common with the people who came before us. We learn from their tragedies and benefit from their triumphs.

In pictures and in words, each of the books in the *Amazing Century* series highlights a different time period in this century. See for yourself. Thumb through the pages of this and all the *Amazing Century* books, and discover the way we were.

The Editors

Lifestyles

Arts and Entertainment

America and the World

Contents

Science and Technology

Sports

Money Matters

Crime, Punishment, and the Law

T I M E L I N E

1980
More than 50
nations join
U.S. boycott of
summer
Olympics
in Moscow

1981
AIDS is first
identified

Sandra Day
O'Connor
is first woman
appointed to
U.S. Supreme
Court

1977
TV drama *Roots*
breaks ratings
records

Star Wars
becomes
blockbuster
movie hit

1975
First personal
computer is
built

1979
Nuclear
accident
occurs at Three
Mile Island
power plant
in Pennsylvania

Antishah
Iranians
storm the
U.S. Embassy
in Iran, taking
more than
60 Americans
hostage

1976
United States
celebrates its
bicentennial

1982
Equal Rights
Amendment
voted down

38th–41st U.S. Presidents

Gerald Ford	Jimmy Carter	

1975	1976	1977	1978	1979	1980	1981	1982

1990

Iraqi forces invade Kuwait, triggering Persian Gulf War

|

Germany reunifies after 45 years

1984

Geraldine Ferraro is first woman candidate for U.S. vice president

1987

Iran-contra hearings take place

|

U.S. stock market collapses

1989

Exxon Valdez spills oil near coast of Alaska

|

Troops crush protesters in China's Tiananmen Square

|

Webster v. Reproductive Health Services decision gives states the right to restrict abortion

|

Communism collapses in Eastern Europe

1991

Persian Gulf War ends

|

Civil Rights Bill outlaws employment decisions based on race, religion, or gender

|

Soviet Union dissolves; Commonwealth of Independent States (CIS) is established by former republics of the Soviet Union

1986

Space shuttle *Challenger* explodes

|

Nuclear accident hits Soviet power plant in Chernobyl

|

News of Iran-contra scandal breaks

1983

U.S. leads invasion of Grenada

Ronald Reagan						George Bush			
1983	1984	1985	1986	1987	1988	1989	1990	1991	1992

Happy Birthday, USA!

July 4, 1976. It was an unforgettable birthday bash. All across the country, Americans celebrated the bicentennial – the 200th anniversary of the birth of the United States of America.

Cities staged celebrations to remind Americans about the Revolutionary War, in which the 13 American colonies won their independence from Great Britain. Most cities held parades. In Los Angeles, the parade was more than 10 miles long. And towns that had existed in 1776 reenacted history. For instance, 20 teams of horse-drawn covered wagons drove through Valley Forge, Pennsylvania, where George Washington's army had spent the third winter of the war. And in Philadelphia, Pennsylvania, at least 1 million people watched a reenactment of the signing of the Declaration of Independence. Then, the cracked Liberty Bell was tapped with a rubber mallet.

Perhaps the grandest celebration took place in New York City. It was called Operation Sail, after the more than 200 sailing ships that moved through the city's harbor. Sixteen of the ships were called the tall ships because they towered more than 125 feet, or 12 stories. Too tall to pass under the Brooklyn Bridge, which spans New York City's East River, they sailed up New York City's Hudson River instead. "It's the most fantastic experience," said one bystander. "Only the United States could do this." ■

The Liberty Bell (below left), which rang when the Declaration of Independence was signed in 1776. Operation Sail (right) in New York City's harbor.

The Camp David Accords

Tension between Israel and its Arab neighbors – Lebanon, Syria, Jordan, and Egypt – has existed since the day Israel became a nation in 1948. Some of that tension was lifted in 1979 with the historic Camp David Accords between Egypt and Israel.

In 1947, the United Nations had divided the area known as Palestine into Jewish and Arab zones. The city of Jerusalem was declared a free city, to be run by an international group. The Jewish zone, called Israel, contained a large amount of territory, including valuable coastline. The Jews accepted the UN arrangement. The Arabs felt the arrangement was unfair and did not accept it. They did not recognize Israel's right to exist.

In 1948, Israel gained its independence. Within 24 hours, Egypt and four other Arab nations invaded Israel. The Israelis drove the Arabs back. They also took over territory that had been in the Arab zone of Palestine. The rest of Arab Palestine was taken over by Egypt and Jordan. As a result, the Palestinians had no land to call their own.

Three Wars and a Peace Treaty

Egypt and other Arab nations remained enemies of Israel for nearly 30 years. Three times – in 1956, 1967, and 1973 – they went to war. The Arab nations lost valuable land to Israel. Even after the fighting stopped, tensions remained high. And the Arab nations still refused to recognize Israel's right to exist.

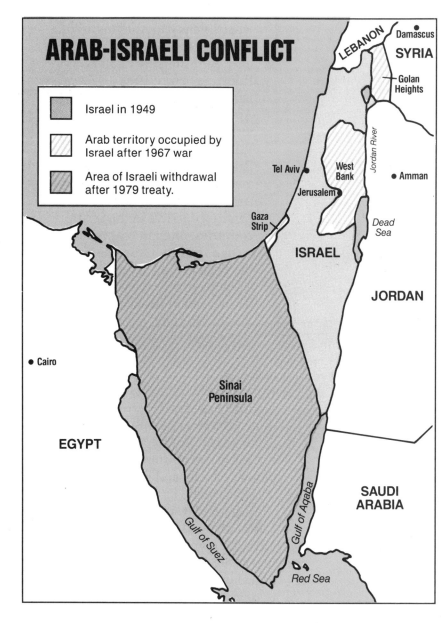

ARAB-ISRAELI CONFLICT

- Israel in 1949
- Arab territory occupied by Israel after 1967 war
- Area of Israeli withdrawal after 1979 treaty.

Damascus
SYRIA
LEBANON
Golan Heights
Jordan River
Tel Aviv
West Bank
Amman
Jerusalem
Gaza Strip
Dead Sea
ISRAEL
JORDAN
Cairo
Sinai Peninsula
EGYPT
SAUDI ARABIA
Gulf of Suez
Gulf of Aqaba
Red Sea

In 1977, Egyptian president Anwar el-Sadat decided that to avoid further loss of lives, Egypt and Israel should be at peace. He visited Israel. He addressed the nation's legislature, saying that their countries should be at

THEN & NOW

In 1991, the United States set up Middle East peace talks. One group present at the talks was Palestinians. Palestinians are the Arabs (or their descendants) who lived in the territory called Palestine before 1948, the year Israel became a state. In the 1948 Arab-Israeli war, Israel overtook much of the Arab zone of Palestine. More than 700,000 Palestinians fled their homeland and became refugees in nearby Arab countries. Most Palestinians continued to live in these Arab countries, often in makeshift refugee camps. Others moved to the Persian Gulf states, where only a few were able to become citizens. Some lived in Israel as citizens of the Jewish state, but were cut off from their former countrymen.

In the 1967 Arab-Israeli war, Israel took over the Gaza Strip and the West Bank (see map on page 7). Many Palestinians lived in these areas. As a result, more than 1 million Arabs came under Israeli rule. The Gaza Strip and the West Bank became known as the "occupied territories" – land under Israeli control, but not officially part of Israel.

Palestinians want to gain control of these occupied territories. The Palestine Liberation Organization (PLO), which represents the Palestinian people, wants to create an independent Palestinian state with Jerusalem as its capital. Although the PLO has tried both military and diplomatic measures, it has not yet gained control of these lands.

peace. Millions of people around the world watched the speech on TV.

Shortly afterward, Israeli prime minister Menachem Begin returned Sadat's visit. But the two leaders could not settle their differences. Peace between Israel and Egypt seemed as far away as ever.

At that point, U.S. president Jimmy Carter stepped in. In September of 1978, he invited Begin and Sadat to meet with him at Camp David, Maryland. The talks lasted for nearly two weeks.

In March of 1979, Sadat and Begin signed the peace treaty known as the Camp David Accords. The treaty was an exchange of peace for land. Egypt agreed to recognize Israel. Israel agreed to return the Sinai Peninsula, land it had won from Egypt in the 1967 war.

Most Americans were pleased with the peace treaty between Israel and Egypt. However, most Arab countries were furious. Arab countries, they felt, should stick together. How dare Sadat make a separate peace with Israel? Why hadn't Sadat demanded a homeland in Israeli-occupied territory for nationless Palestinians? Angered by Sadat's policy toward Israel, a group of gunmen killed Sadat in 1981. ■

The Camp David Accords were a historic peace agreement between two longtime enemies. If you could create a peace agreement between any two countries today, which countries would you choose? What compromises would you ask each country to make? Why?

NEW YORK, TUESDAY, MARCH 27, 1979

VOL.CXXVIII .... No.44,169   Copyright © 1979 The New York Times

EGYPT AND ISRAEL SIGN FORMAL TREATY, ENDING A STATE OF WAR AFTER 30 YEARS; SADAT AND BEGIN PRAISE CARTER'S ROLE

PEC PARLEY WEIGHS

CEREMONY IS FESTIVE

Accord on Sinai Oil Opens Way to the First Peace in Mideast Dispute

A Human Rights President

Jimmy Carter was elected president in 1976. A former governor of Georgia, he was considered a political "outsider" – not part of the Washington, D.C., political scene. Carter was a deeply religious man. He promised to bring honesty back to government. "I'll never tell a lie," he said.

Once in office, Carter stressed the importance of human rights worldwide. He criticized other governments for jailing people without a trial and for torturing prisoners. For this reason, he cut off military aid to several Central and South American countries, including El Salvador, Argentina, and Brazil. These countries were friendly to the United States, but Carter objected to their mistreatment of citizens who disagreed with government policies. He also praised Soviet citizens who were jailed for speaking out against their government.

Anwar Sadat (left), Menachem Begin (center), and Jimmy Carter at the Camp David Summit.

Revolution in Iran

Iran – an oil-rich country on the Persian Gulf – was an important U.S. ally before 1979. In that year, however, events in Iran shocked the United States and the rest of the world.

By 1979, Shah Mohammad Reza Pahlavi had ruled Iran for more than 30 years. The shah had supporters within Iran, but he also had many critics. Supporters liked his attempts to make the country more modern. For instance, he gave women the right to vote. He let Iranian youths study in the United States. He broke up large estates and gave the land to small farmers.

The shah's critics, however, called these changes "forced westernization." Iran's religious leaders felt that some of the reforms went against Islamic laws.

Also, many of the shah's officials were corrupt, and his secret police tortured and killed people who opposed him.

In 1978, riots against the shah broke out in the capital city of Teheran. To show support for the rioters, workers shut down the nation's oil fields. The country was coming unglued.

In January of 1979, the shah fled Iran. Soon, religious leader Ayatollah Ruhollah Khomeini returned from exile in France. In triumph, he set up a religious government. He condemned the United States for supporting the shah, calling America a "stubborn, spoiled child" and the "great Satan."

The Hostage Crisis

In October of 1979, the shah entered an American hospital to be treated for

Mohammad Reza Pahlavi (left), the Shah of Iran, and Empress Farah. In 1979, Ayatollah Ruhollah Khomeini (right) seized power.

cancer. Antishah Iranians were furious that the United States welcomed him. On November 4, they broke into the American embassy in Teheran and took more than 60 Americans as hostages. The terrorists made angry demands; for one, they demanded that the United States return the shah to Iran to be tried for "crimes against the Iranian people."

President Carter would not meet their demands. Instead, he cut off all trade with Iran. In reply, the Iranians paraded the blindfolded hostages in front of cheering crowds as angry Americans watched the scene on TV.

The hostage crisis dragged on. In April of 1980, the United States attempted a rescue by helicopter. But several of the helicopters broke down in the Iranian desert, and eight American crewmen died. The rescue mission was a failure.

Meanwhile, President Carter kept negotiating. But the Iranian government refused to release the hostages. The crisis became an important issue in the 1980 presidential race between Carter and Ronald Reagan. Experts agree that

Iranians parading American hostages (top) through the streets of Teheran in 1979. The freed hostages (left) returning home in January 1981.

Carter's failure to obtain the hostages' release helped cause him to lose the election.

For the last two months of his presidency, Carter kept trying to deal with Iran. Finally, the United States met some of the terrorists' demands. Iran agreed to release the hostages. But it did not do so until 33 minutes after President Reagan took his oath of office on January 20, 1981. The hostages had been held captive for 444 days. ■

The U.S. in Central America

U.S. soldiers after the invasion of Grenada.

Since 1904, the United States has claimed a right to help keep order in Latin America. In the 1980s, the United States tried to exercise that right in several Latin American countries, including Grenada and Nicaragua.

Grenada

Grenada is a tiny island nation off the northern coast of South America. In 1979, a new government came to power there. Over the next few years, it developed close ties with Communist Cuba. In October of 1983, Grenada's prime minister, Maurice Bishop, was killed during a military takeover.

President Reagan ordered American troops to invade Grenada. The invasion, he said, would "restore democracy" to Grenada and protect the 1,000 or so Americans there. Reagan said he feared they might be hurt or taken hostage by the new government.

After the invasion, the pro-Communist leaders were placed under arrest. U.S. and Caribbean peacekeeping forces were gradually withdrawn. A general election in December 1984 established a democratic government on the island.

Nicaragua

During the 1970s, revolution broke out in Nicaragua. The revolutionaries called themselves the Sandinista National Liberation Front. The Sandinistas opposed Nicaraguan dictator Anastasio Somoza Debayle, who had done little to help the country's poor. By 1979, the Sandinistas were strong enough to force Somoza to resign. The Sandinistas said their goal was to provide good health care, housing, education, and jobs for all Nicaraguans.

The revolution had left Nicaragua in very poor shape. The United States

Lt. Col. Oliver North (left) being sworn in at the Iran-contra hearings in 1987. North was involved in illegally sending aid to the Nicaraguan contras (right).

sent nearly $100 million in aid. But the United States was not comfortable with the Sandinistas, who delayed holding national elections and who began to grow closer to Cuba and the Soviet Union.

When Ronald Reagan became president, he changed U.S. policy toward Nicaragua. He cut off economic aid to the country and tried to prevent other countries from trading with Nicaragua. Reagan claimed the Sandinistas were Communists. He also began sending money to an anti-Sandinista group known as the *contras*. Reagan called the contras "freedom fighters." By 1983, the U.S. Central Intelligence Agency (CIA) was helping to train contra soldiers.

Many Americans criticized Reagan's policy. They pointed out that the Nicaraguan people did not support the contras. Most contra leaders had belonged to Somoza's corrupt government. And when the CIA helped plant explosives in Nicaraguan

harbors, the World Court decided that the United States was in the wrong.

Despite the criticism, Reagan continued funding and training the contras. After a point, Congress voted against sending the contras more money. So the Reagan administration secretly obtained money from private citizens and the governments of Saudi Arabia, Taiwan, and Brunei. These funds were sent to the contras. Because Congress had passed a law against funding the contras, this was illegal.

The Iran-Contra Affair

Americans soon learned that more laws had been broken. In November of 1986, the Iran-contra scandal was revealed. The United States had been secretly selling weapons to the Iranian

Central American presidents signing a peace agreement. The agreement led to free elections in Nicaragua.

government. The aim was to get Iranian help for the release of American hostages in Lebanon. This went against the U.S. policy of not bargaining with terrorists *or* aiding Iran in its war with Iraq. A few weeks later, Americans learned that millions of dollars of profits from the arms sale had been sent secretly – illegally – to the Nicaraguan contras.

Two investigations were held – one by a group of citizens and the other by Congress. Both investigations criticized President Reagan for allowing government officials to carry out illegal actions in secret. Helping the contras did not justify breaking the law, the

investigators said. Several members of the Reagan administration were charged with crimes – lying to Congress, destroying official documents, accepting bribes – and some were convicted.

From War to a Truce

In 1987, Nicaragua's neighbors decided to help solve the crisis in Nicaragua. Led by Costa Rican president Oscar Arias Sánchez, five Central American nations drew up a peace plan. The Sandinistas and the contras were to sign a truce. Nicaragua would then hold a free election to choose its new government.

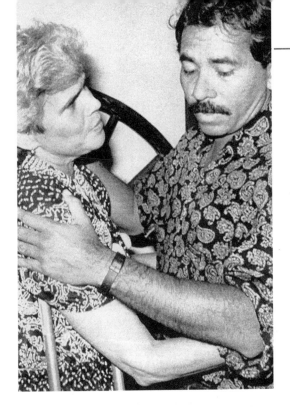

The election took place in February of 1990. The Nicaraguan people elected Violeta Barrios de Chamorro as president. President Chamorro's election ended 11 years of Sandinista rule in Nicaragua. ■

Do you think the United States had the right to invade Grenada? To support the Nicaraguan contras? Under what circumstances does a country have the right to get involved in other countries' affairs?

Nicaraguan President Daniel Ortega Saavedra (right) congratulating Violeta Chamorro (left) after Chamorro defeated him in the presidential elections.

The Sanctuary Movement

Between 1980 and 1982, thousands of people left their war-torn homeland of El Salvador. Most went to Mexico or Honduras. But more than 100,000 tried to enter the United States.

The Reagan administration refused to let them in. To be admitted, refugees had to be victims of human-rights violations, such as being tortured or being jailed without trial. The administration said that the Salvadorans were not running for their lives; instead, it said, they were just looking for jobs.

The refugees disagreed. El Salvador was in the middle of a bloody civil war. The right-wing government had murdered about 22,000 civilians in 1980 alone.

Nevertheless, the Reagan administration sent the refugees back to El Salvador. At the same time, it continued to send hundreds of millions of dollars to El Salvador's government. The Reagan administration insisted that the government was only trying to put down a Communist uprising.

In 1982, five churches in the United States announced that they would provide shelter, food, clothing, and money to refugees from El Salvador and Guatemala – even if the refugees were in the United States illegally. "What we're doing is simply what the faith compels us to do," said the Rev. John A. Fife of the Southside Presbyterian Church in Tucson, Arizona. By 1985, the sanctuary movement had spread to more than 250 churches and synagogues across the country.

In 1991, a lawsuit supported by 80 immigrants' rights and church groups was settled out of court. The settlement said that the U.S. government should not turn back refugees from El Salvador and Guatemala. From that point on, refugees could ask for sanctuary without fear of being sent back to Central America.

Abolishing Apartheid

Nelson Mandela speaking at a rally. Mandela was released after spending 27 years in a South African prison.

"**A**mandla! Amandla! i-Afrika, mayibuye!" ("Power! Power! Africa, it is ours!")

The date was February 11, 1990. The place was Cape Town, South Africa. The speaker was Nelson Mandela. He had just been released from a South African prison after 27 years. Why had he been jailed? Because he had openly opposed South Africa's policy of *apartheid*, or racial separation.

South Africa had adopted apartheid as its official policy in 1948. Under apartheid, South Africans were divided into four groups: whites, blacks, Asians, and coloreds—people of mixed ancestry. Each group had to live in its own areas, study in its own schools, and worship in its own churches. Although only about 15 percent of the population was white, whites held the best jobs with the highest pay. They owned all of the farmland. They were also the only ones allowed to vote.

Strict laws prevented most social contact between the races. Apartheid was also enforced through "pass" laws. All nonwhites had to carry a pass, or identity card. They could not enter white areas without it. If they did not show it when asked to, they were arrested and fined. Many were also beaten and jailed.

The government of South Africa shut down newspapers that opposed apartheid. It declared Mandela's organization, the African National Congress (ANC), illegal. Police could enter homes without a warrant. They could jail people without a trial. People who spoke against the government were banned. That meant they could not leave their homes at night, on weekends, or on holidays. They could meet with only one person at a time.

Over the years, black South Africans, together with some whites, protested against apartheid. Sometimes they used violence, blowing up white-owned office buildings and shops and raiding white-owned farms. In the 1980s, they held nationwide strikes. More than 1 million workers took part in a 1988 strike.

Many Americans were horrified by apartheid and wanted our government to take action to end it. Many American businesses and universities stopped investing in South African companies. In 1986, the U.S. government put economic sanctions on South Africa. This meant that

South Africans celebrating Nelson Mandela's release from prison.

American companies could not trade with South Africa.

In 1989, F. W. de Klerk became president of South Africa. President de Klerk decided to do away with apartheid as official policy. "One cannot build security on injustice," he said. One by one, the laws that separated the people of South Africa were done away with. Nonwhites no longer had to carry passes. They could live anywhere they wanted to. The African National Congress and other black political organizations became legal. The government released more than 900 political prisoners in addition to Mandela.

In June of 1991, President de Klerk announced that he would soon start working on a new constitution that would give black people equal voting rights. In July, President Bush lifted the U.S. economic sanctions on South Africa. He said it was "the right thing to do in order to encourage continued change. . . ." Many Americans felt that his decision was made too soon, however. ◼

Stephen Biko was an anti-apartheid activist who died in a South African jail in the late 1970s. The movie Cry Freedom *tells his story. Rent the movie, or borrow it from your public library.*

The END of an EMPIRE

ESTONIA
LATVIA
LITHUANIA
● Moscow
BYELORUSSIA
UKRAINE
MOLDAVIA
GEORGIA
ARMENIA
AZERBAIJAN
TURKMENISTAN
UZBEKISTAN
KAZAKH REPUBLIC
KIRGHIZ REPUBLIC
TADJIKISTAN
Caspian Sea
SIBERIA
RUSSIAN REPUBLIC

THE SOVIET REPUBLICS

Mikhail Gorbachev (top), the last president of the Soviet Union, resigned in 1991. The map shows the 15 republics of the Soviet Union before 1991.

"The old Union of Soviet Socialist Republics is no more," announced the news magazines in the summer of 1991. That summer, the collapse of communism in the USSR signaled the end of an empire.

And what an empire it was. Since 1922, when the Soviet Union was formed, the USSR had forced many of its neighbors into the union. The union was held together by economics (communism), by force (the Soviet army), and by fear (the secret service, or KGB). Other Eastern European countries fell under Soviet influence and practiced communism as well. For nearly 70 years, the USSR was a major world power. In the late 1980s, however, the union began to dissolve.

Glasnost and Perestroika

In 1985, new Soviet leader Mikhail Gorbachev realized that his country faced many economic and political problems. He began to make sweeping changes. He called them *glasnost* and *perestroika*.

Glasnost means "openness." Under glasnost, Soviet citizens received rights they had not had before. For example, they were allowed to speak out against government policies. They could form non-Communist political parties. They were allowed to travel freely from one city to another and from the Soviet Union to other countries.

Perestroika means "restructuring." Gorbachev planned to restructure the Soviet economic system. He tried to change what goods were produced, who made the decisions, and who owned certain businesses. That is, he began shifting the decision making and ownership from the central government to the citizens.

One result of glasnost and perestroika was a new attitude. Many of the 15 republics that made up the Soviet Union began demanding more control over their own governments. Some republics declared their independence. And Boris Yeltsin, president of the Russian Republic (the largest and richest republic), urged Gorbachev to move faster in his reforms.

The Attempted Coup

But Gorbachev did not move fast enough. No one was pleased with his timing: the reformers said he moved too slowly; the Communist hard-liners thought he moved too quickly. On August 18, 1991, some of these hard-liners staged a coup — an attempt to overthrow the government. They placed Gorbachev under arrest in his vacation home. They sent the army to attack the government building in which Yeltsin was protected by citizens and some of the military. The army refused to attack. It became clear that Soviet citizens did not favor the coup.

Russian Republic President Boris Yeltsin addressing the Russian parliament.

After three days, the coup failed. Gorbachev returned; the coup leaders were arrested. The coup seemed to be the last gasp of the old-rule Communists.

The New Commonwealth

Other Soviet republics began to declare their independence while Gorbachev struggled to preserve the crumbling union. As the republics broke away, Gorbachev lost his power base. At the same time, Yeltsin gained ground as the leader of the reform movement.

On December 8, 1991, three republics—Russia, Byelorussia (Belarus), and Ukraine—founded a new *commonwealth*, or political unit. This group, the Commonwealth of Independent States (CIS), became recognized as the legal successor to the Soviet Union. In late December 1991, all power of the central Soviet government was transferred to the countries of the new commonwealth. No one was sure what the new commonwealth would be like. But one thing was sure. As one former Soviet citizen said, "The old union does not exist, and there can be no return to it."

Changes in Eastern Europe

Outside the Soviet Union, countries under Communist rule also changed due to glasnost and perestroika. The Communist governments of Eastern Europe had been supported by the

All power of the central Soviet government was transferred to the countries of the new commonwealth.

USSR – and the Soviet army – for decades. In 1989, however, Gorbachev announced that the Soviet army would no longer help these Communist leaders stay in power. Soon, these countries went through tremendous changes.

East Germany. After World War II, Germany had been divided into two countries: West Germany, with a free market; and East Germany, which practiced communism. The city of Berlin was divided as well. Many Germans tried to flee from East to West Germany. To stop this flow of refugees, the government of East Germany built the Berlin Wall in 1961.

By 1989, East Germany was in trouble. Its economy was in shambles. The government was more unpopular than ever. Citizens began demonstrating against the government. Pressure mounted. Finally, the East German cabinet resigned. The new government promised free elections. It also allowed East Germans to cross the Berlin Wall.

Soon, German citizens began tearing down the Berlin Wall. In March of 1990, East Germans voted the Communist government out of office. In October, East and West Germany became reunified – they became a single nation once again.

Poland. Since 1980, a labor group called Solidarity had opposed the Communist government. In 1989, the government finally agreed to hold free elections. Solidarity put up candidates to run against the Communist party candidates. Solidarity's candidates won. The next year, Lech Walesa, Solidarity's leader, was chosen president.

Czechoslovakia. The Communist government collapsed after hundreds of thousands of people demonstrated against it. The new president, Vaclav Havel, was a playwright who had opposed the Communists for years.

Hungary. The Communist party itself voted to give up communism.

Romania. The citizens rose up, captured, and killed the Communist dictator Nicolae Ceausescu.

Bulgaria. The Communist leader resigned in November 1989. Free elections were set for the following year.

Albania. The government allowed non-Communist parties to run candidates for office. The new government had a majority of non-Communists.

The sweeping changes taking place in both Eastern Europe and the Soviet Union amazed most Americans. President Bush had the new democracies in mind when he coined the phrase "New World Order." ■

In the early 1980s, President Reagan called the Soviet Union an "evil empire." Americans have viewed the Communist nations of Europe as our enemy ever since World War II. Now that communism seems to have collapsed, how do you view these nations? Do you think that the United States should send them aid? Do you think that they still pose a threat to the world?

Tiananmen Square

For seven weeks in the spring of 1989, it seemed as if communism might collapse in China as well as in Europe. In April, Chinese students began demonstrating for reforms. Tiananmen Square, in the capital, Beijing, soon became the center of the daily demonstrations. The students asked for democracy. They wanted more say in the government. They wanted freedom of speech and of the press. They wanted to be able to choose their jobs instead of being told by the government what jobs to take. Workers and other groups throughout the country also began demonstrating for change.

The Communist government cracked down. On the night of June 3, it sent troops and tanks into Tiananmen Square. The soldiers killed hundreds – perhaps thousands – of unarmed students. Over the next few weeks, the government arrested thousands of people and killed many of them. The democracy movement was crushed. ■

A 19-year-old Chinese citizen stopping a column of tanks headed toward Tiananmen Square. The photo was taken by an amateur photographer – from a hiding place.

War in the Gulf

The trouble began on August 2, 1990. Under Saddam Hussein, the dictator of Iraq, Iraqi troops invaded neighboring Kuwait. Iraq had been claiming for years that part of Kuwait actually belonged to Iraq. In addition, Hussein had just ended an eight-year war with Iran. He wanted Kuwait's oil to help him pay off Iraq's debts from that war.

Hussein's invasion of Kuwait posed a threat to Saudi Arabia. Saudi Arabia, an ally of the United States, contains almost one-third of the world's known oil reserves. Some people feared that if Saddam Hussein controlled all that oil, he might raise oil prices. Americans would have to pay much more for gasoline, heating oil, fertilizers, plastics, and other goods made from oil.

Iraqi President Saddam Hussein (left) and U.S. President George Bush.

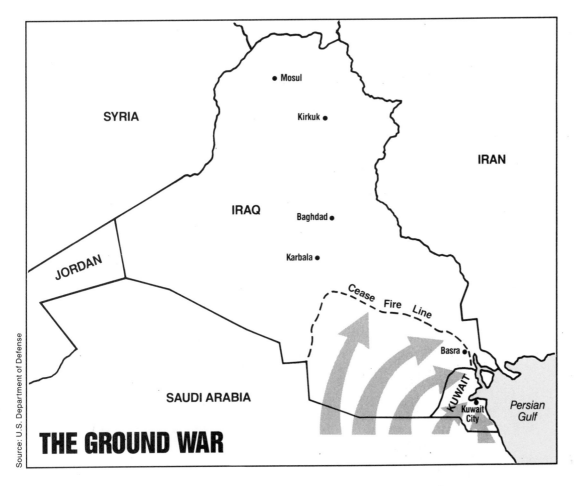

Source: U.S. Department of Defense

THE GROUND WAR

The map shows the land invasion of Iraq and Kuwait by the U.S. and its allies.

Operation Desert Shield

President Bush told Saddam Hussein to withdraw Iraqi troops from Kuwait by January 15, 1991. The invasion "will not stand," the president said.

Bush won the support of the United Nations. The UN imposed economic sanctions against Iraq, cutting off its trade. The UN also agreed to send in troops if Hussein did not meet the deadline.

Bush also got the backing of the U.S. Congress. Senators and representatives debated the issue for three days. Some favored the use of force. Others urged the United States to "slowly strangle Saddam with sanctions." Finally, on January 12, Congress voted to give Bush authority to go to war. "This is the best chance for peace," said Senator Robert Dole.

Operation Desert Storm

The air war against Iraq started on January 16, 1991. Thirty-seven days later, on February 23, the ground war began. Just 100 hours later, on February 27, President Bush announced a cease-fire. Operation Desert Storm was a success.

While fewer than 150 Americans had been killed in the fighting, Iraq had lost up to 100,000 soldiers. Most of its power lines and telephone circuits had been destroyed. Drinking water was unsanitary. Doctors feared that this could lead to the spread of deadly diseases such as cholera and typhoid. Some doctors estimated that tens of thousands of Iraqi civilians would die by the end of 1991.

Although he had lost the war, Saddam Hussein remained in power. He had enough soldiers and weapons

left to put down two uprisings against his rule. One, in northern Iraq, was led by Iraqi Kurds. About 1 million Kurds fled Iraq and became refugees in Turkey and Iran. The other uprising, in southern Iraq, was of Shiite Muslims. About 700,000 Shiite Muslims fled to Iran.

Saddam Hussein also created a serious environmental problem. Before

Scenes of the 1991 Persian Gulf War. From top: a U.S. aircraft carrier; U.S. soldiers; surrendering Iraqi soldiers; Iraqi vehicles under attack by Allied forces as they try to flee Kuwait.

Warspeak

The gulf war popularized a lot of military terms. Here are some of the common words and phrases:
• Scud: Soviet-made missile used by Iraq
• Patriot: U.S. Army missile designed to stop the Scud
• Take out: kill
• Collateral damage: civilians killed by weapons aimed at military targets
• K-Day: the day the allies invaded Kuwait
• Fur ball: a fight between airplanes
• Sortie: a single attack by a single plane
• Bogie: an enemy plane

Iraqi soldiers left Kuwait, they wrecked or set fire to the country's 1,000 oil wells. The thick, black smoke from the fires spread over Kuwait, causing thousands of people to become sick. In addition, oil kept gushing from wells that were no longer burning. The oil soaked into the ground and killed wildlife along the shore. Some of the oil began catching fire. The fires raged for nearly nine months. ■

Some Americans think the United Nations forces did not do enough in Iraq. They think Saddam Hussein should have been overthrown.

Do you agree? Should the UN have gone beyond its goal of freeing Kuwait?

What do you think of the United States' role in the Persian Gulf War?

General Colin Powell (left) and General H. Norman Schwarzkopf.

Two Generals

General Colin Powell

In August of 1989, General Colin L. Powell became chairman of the Joint Chiefs of Staff. He was the first African-American, and the youngest man, ever named to that position. As chairman, Powell was the president's main military adviser. He was responsible for preparing plans for war. When the gulf war broke out, General Powell was in charge of directing the fighting.

Colin Powell grew up in the poor South Bronx neighborhood of New York City. His Jamaican parents encouraged him to get an education. After graduating from high school, Powell attended the City College of New York. There, he joined the Reserve Officers Training Corps (ROTC). "In my second year of ROTC," he said, "I realized, 'Hey, this is fun, and you do it well.'" After graduating from college, he began his

military career, serving in West Germany and in the Vietnam War. As chairman of the Joint Chiefs of Staff, Powell was in the spotlight during the Persian Gulf War.

General H. Norman Schwarzkopf

The biggest hero of the gulf war was the American field commander, General H. Norman Schwarzkopf, also known as "Stormin' Norman." General Schwarzkopf served two tours of duty in Vietnam during the 1960s. There, he became known for risking his own life to help others. He was awarded three Silver Star medals for his courage in battle.

General Schwarzkopf retired from the army in the fall of 1991. More than any other person, he helped restore respect for military leaders among Americans – respect that those leaders had lost during the Vietnam War.

Minority Voices

"In the 21st century—and that's not far off—racial and ethnic groups in the United States will outnumber whites for the first time," reported *Time* magazine in 1990. Growing in numbers, America's minority groups will most likely grow in power as well. African-Americans, Hispanics, Asians, Native Americans, and other minority groups will have a greater voice in the government. But not for the first time. In the 1950s and 1960s, the civil rights movement took steps toward empowering minorities. Since then, minority voices have been heard from politics to education to culture.

Politics

In the 1980s, civil rights leader Reverend Jesse Jackson struggled to give blacks and other minorities a greater voice. He called for a "rainbow coalition"—blacks working with other minorities and women to gain more power in America. In 1984, Jackson ran for the Democratic party's presidential nomination. "If you run, you might lose," he said. "If you don't run, you're guaranteed to lose." Jackson did not win the nomination. But his campaign was a success in other ways: as the first African-American to run a full-scale campaign for president,

The Reverend Jesse Jackson, a Democratic presidential candidate in 1984 and 1988.

Jackson succeeded in bringing a minority voice to national politics.

Jackson's vision of a "rainbow coalition" has its problems, however. Minority groups do not always agree on issues. And they often compete with each other for political power. For instance, Chicago's Hispanic leaders shift their support between black leaders and white leaders, depending on which group will help the Hispanic community at that time. "If you're thinking of power," said one Hispanic community leader, "you don't put your eggs in one basket."

Native Americans

The situation of Native Americans, or American Indians, is unique among American minority groups. Native Americans have lived on this continent for centuries. When Europeans began to settle in North America, they pushed the Indians off the land. Eventually, Native Americans were forced onto reservations, lands set aside for them by the government.

In the 1970s and 1980s, many Native Americans lived in poverty. Many reservations had high unemployment rates, low education levels, and an alarming rate of alcohol abuse. But at the same time, Indian groups began to voice pride in their heritage. They lobbied for religious and cultural freedom. And they worked to improve conditions on the reservations. In the 1980s, several tribes made very successful business moves – some by using the natural resources found on their reservations.

Native Americans also have high hopes for their future. Said Wilma Mankiller, Cherokee Nation principal chief, "The dreams of our people are woven from a tragic past and difficult present. Yet those dreams have the ability to continue to guide our people to hope and work for a positive future."

Education

Minority groups have also gained a greater voice in the field of education. In 1988, President Reagan appointed Lauro F. Cavazos, a Hispanic-American, as U.S. secretary of education. And in the 1980s, Bolivian

Wilma Mankiller, principal chief of the Cherokee Nation.

immigrant Jaime Escalante earned nationwide respect for his work with Hispanic high school students in East Los Angeles. Escalante became famous when *Stand and Deliver*—a movie about the struggles of Escalante and his students—was released in 1987.

Minority voices have affected what is taught in schools as well. In the 1970s and 1980s, educators argued about *whose* history and culture should be taught: The history of the white settlers of the United States? Of the blacks who were brought here as slaves? Of the minority groups who immigrated here? These and other questions about education have yet to be answered.

Culture

As minority groups grow larger, their customs and lifestyles influence "mainstream" America. For instance, in Miami, Florida, businesspeople often must speak both English and Spanish to communicate with their customers. And Americans often come face to face with a variety of cultures. Consider this example: at a Houston, Texas, restaurant, the owner, a Korean immigrant, trains Hispanic immigrant workers to make Chinese-style food for the customers, many of whom are black. As college professor Molefi Asante said to *Time*, "Today, America is a [sampling] of the world." ∎

Should ethnic minorities be encouraged to "blend in" with American society? Or should they hold onto their own customs and languages? Give reasons to support your opinion.

The movie Stand and Deliver *tells the story of Jaime Escalante and his students. Rent the video, or check it out from your public library.*

Math teacher Jaime Escalante (right) is well known for his work with Hispanic high school students.

Women's Issues

The late 1970s and the 1980s were years of both setbacks and successes for the women's rights movement. A big setback was the defeat of the Equal Rights Amendment (ERA). The ERA, a proposed addition to the Constitution, would have assured that women had rights equal to men's. But by the 1982 deadline, not enough states had voted for the ERA, so it did not become law.

Although the ERA was defeated, women made important gains during those years. Because of legal and political battles they won, women could take action on job discrimination, sexual harassment, child-support payments, and insurance policies. Women also gained political power: in 1984, Geraldine Ferraro, then a U.S. Congresswoman, became the first female candidate for U.S. vice president.

Women's groups say that there are still fights to be won. One pressing issue is salary: in the late 1980s, working women still earned only two-thirds as much as men working in the same jobs. ■

Women's Rights Legislation, 1978-1991

1978 Amendment to 1964 Civil Rights Act: Banned job discrimination because of pregnancy. Required that health and disability plans cover pregnant workers.

1984 Retirement Equity Act: Ensured a pension for homemakers whose spouses died before reaching retirement.

1988 National Women's Business Council created to oversee government assistance of women-owned businesses.

1991 Civil Rights Bill: Outlawed employment decisions based on gender, race, religion. Allowed money (damages) for victims of harassment and discrimination.

Feminist leaders and former First Ladies Rosalynn Carter and Betty Ford gathering at the 1977 National Women's Conference in Houston.

That Old-Time Religion

Newsweek magazine called 1976 "The Year of the Evangelicals." Evangelicals are Christians who believe in preaching the gospel of Jesus Christ to the world. Many say they have had a "born again" experience or a "spiritual rebirth"—a deep personal experience of Jesus. According to a poll, there were 40 million Evangelical Christians in America in 1976—and one of them was elected president that year: former Georgia governor Jimmy Carter.

Evangelical Christianity had been common in America during the 19th century. Many people believed that the Bible was true as history and science. But in the 20th century, Evangelical Christianity became less popular.

Why did the old-time religion make a comeback in the 1970s? The Vietnam War, high divorce rates, legalized abortion, Watergate—all these events made people think America was breaking down. People were looking for the tried-and-true beliefs that Americans seemed to have lost. Some people found meaning in the old-time religion.

The Televangelists

Evangelists like Billy Graham and Oral Roberts had been preaching to large audiences for years. But the 1970s saw a new kind of religious leader, the "televangelists," who used television to reach millions of people. One of the better known was Pat Robertson, who had founded the Christian Broadcasting Network in 1960.

Robertson and other televangelists used other new ways to spread their message. In addition to using radio and

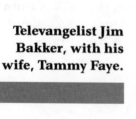

Televangelist Jim Bakker, with his wife, Tammy Faye.

television, they also started Christian schools and universities. They sold children's Bible books and filmstrips and sent out mass mailings to raise money. Jim Bakker founded Heritage Village USA, a Christian theme park.

The Moral Majority

By the late 1970s, Evangelical Christians had turned to politics. In 1979, the Reverend Jerry Falwell of the "Old Time Gospel Hour" formed the Moral Majority. Falwell wanted to "rally together the people of this country who still believe in decency, the home, the family, morality, the free enterprise system, and all the great ideals that are the cornerstone of this nation." The Moral Majority opposed abortion, divorce, pornography, and homosexuality. It favored prayer in public schools and wanted schools to teach "creation science"—the biblical story of creation—along with the theory of evolution. Its members believed it was their duty to vote for candidates who agreed with their moral beliefs. The Moral Majority strongly supported Ronald Reagan in the 1980 presidential election. Falwell claimed some credit when Reagan was elected president.

Some people felt that the Moral Majority was trying to force its views on other Americans. Still, the

Evangelical movement grew as a political movement. In 1988, Pat Robertson ran for president as a Republican candidate and did well in several primary elections.

The televangelists, however, ran into trouble as the 1980s ended. Jim Bakker was involved in a sex scandal. Later, in 1988, he was convicted of fraud in raising money for Heritage Village USA. Instead of using the money to run the company, he used it for himself and his family. He received a long prison sentence, and he and his wife, Tammy Faye, lost many of their followers. Another popular TV preacher, Jimmy Swaggart, admitted he had made advances to a prostitute. Amid a drop in membership and contributions, Jerry Falwell left the Moral Majority to return to full-time preaching. By the early 1990s, millions of Americans still were Evangelicals. But the movement seemed to be losing steam as a force in American politics. ■

The Reverend Jerry Falwell (above left) talking with President Reagan. The Reverend Jimmy Swaggart (right) speaking at a press conference after the media learned of his affair with a prostitute.

What is your opinion of the Moral Majority's involvement in politics? Do you feel that religious ties could help or hurt a political candidate? In general, do you think that church leaders should be actively involved in politics? Give reasons to support your opinion.

The Changing American Family

Weekend fathers, latchkey kids, supermom, superdad, Mr. Mom – America needed new words like these to describe the changing families of the 1970s and 1980s. By the 1980s, the "traditional family" – breadwinner father, homemaker mother, and children – seemed to be breaking down in the United States.

The facts are clear:

Divorce. In 1991, experts estimated that up to half of all new marriages would end in divorce.

Single Mothers. In 1987, more than 25 percent of births were to single mothers. That was a huge increase from 1970 (less than 11 percent) and 1950 (4 percent).

The result? Between 1970 and 1988, the number of single-parent families more than doubled. Nearly one-fourth of all children under 18 lived with just one parent by 1988. Half of the children born in the 1980s will live with one parent for part of their lives. And single parenthood often means poverty. By the mid-1980s, 54 percent of single-parent families earned less than $10,989 per year – that is, they lived below the poverty line.

Working Parents. In many two-parent families, both parents work outside the home. Parents must juggle both jobs and family. And children are often left in the care of grandparents, babysitters, or daycare centers. Or they become "latchkey kids," children who stay home alone after school.

Trends in Marriage. Many Americans are marrying later in life. That means

CHANGING TIMES

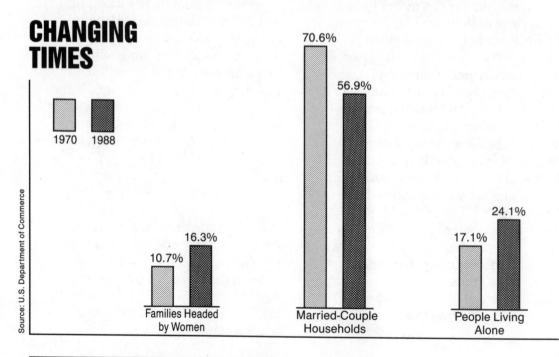

Source: U.S. Department of Commerce

1970   1988

Families Headed by Women: 10.7% / 16.3%

Married-Couple Households: 70.6% / 56.9%

People Living Alone: 17.1% / 24.1%

having children later—and, often, having fewer children than their own parents had.

Others are not marrying at all. The marriage rate in 1989 was lower than it had been since 1970. Some prefer a career to marriage. Some prefer to live with a partner without getting married. Others remain single after a divorce or the death of a spouse. Whatever the reason, the trend toward staying single—along with the trends in divorce, single motherhood, and working parents—is helping to create a new kind of family. ■

In recent years, singles have begun to demand some of the privileges married people have. For instance, unmarried people want to be able to put their live-in lovers on their insurance policies. Gays have been demanding the right to have same-sex marriages. Some people support changes like these; others do not. Ask a few friends and co-workers how they feel. Then, write up the results of your informal survey.

"Latchkey kids" stay home alone after school because their parents have daytime jobs.

The Graying of America

In 1988, President Ronald Reagan turned 77 years old. In his spare time, he rode horses and chopped wood. It was no surprise that the president of the United States was long past the usual retirement age. Many Americans were over 65 – and often not acting their age.

The population of older people in the United States is climbing fast. In 1900, only 4 percent of Americans were older than age 65. By 1990, nearly 13 percent of Americans were 65 and over – and that number will climb to more than 17 percent by the year 2020. Older people are also healthier than the elderly of the past: in 1988, half of America's senior citizens aged 75 to 84 reported no health problems that limit their activities.

Why are people living longer and staying healthier? Many people eat better, get better medical care, are in

Members of the Gray Panthers, a senior citizens' group, demonstrating for changes in government policies.

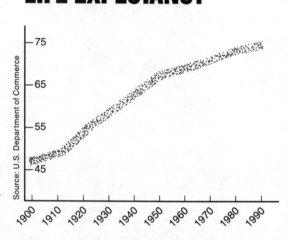

CHANGE IN LIFE EXPECTANCY

Source: U.S. Department of Commerce

75
65
55
45

1900 1910 1920 1930 1940 1950 1960 1970 1980 1990

better physical condition, and have a better outlook on life than in years past. Aging does take its toll on the body. But studies show that proper diet and exercise can lengthen life – and make it healthier. And seniors are doing just what the doctor ordered. A recent poll showed that nearly half of Americans over 65 exercise regularly.

But the aging of America has also created problems. One example: the problems involved with the Social Security system.

The Social Security Act became law in 1935. Under this law, the government takes some money from each worker's paychecks and pays some of it back when the worker retires. Social Security checks are given each month to retirees, disabled persons, and families of workers who have died – nearly 40 million people by 1990. Social Security has helped many Americans buy food and clothing and

pay medical bills that they could not afford otherwise.

But in the 1970s, it became more expensive to run the Social Security program. By 1982, the program had almost no money left. There was talk about stopping Social Security, but many Americans wanted it to continue. President Reagan and Congress passed laws in 1983 to raise money and changed some of the rules to prevent another money shortage.

The cost of Social Security will continue to rise as people live longer. Medical costs are higher for those who live longer. And the program will have to pay benefits to even more elderly people in the years ahead. The "baby boom" generation – those born between the late 1940s and 1960 – is the largest generation of people ever born in the United States. When this generation retires, there will be fewer workers to support the large number of Social Security payments. Then the money must come from the federal budget.

There is another problem created by our aging society. Some families have to take care of elderly parents who are unable to take care of themselves. This can create a strain when these families are still raising their children. Such people are sometimes called the "sandwich" generation – between two generations who need their support. ■

A 70-year-old Virginia man displaying the gold medals he won at the 1989 Senior Olympics.

THEN & NOW

In the past, TV and movies portrayed older people as senile, childish, or especially wise. Today, seniors have a different image. TV and movies show them living life to the fullest. For example, TV's "The Golden Girls" shows middle-aged and elderly women who try new things, enjoy themselves, and have fulfilling sex lives.

Seniors themselves have brought about this image change. Older Americans played an important part in the "fitness craze" of the 1970s and 1980s.

Some, like 74-year-old James Jay, run marathons. Others are more daring: Hulda Crooks climbed more than 90 mountains after she reached the age of 65. Many more continue to work part-time or do volunteer work after their retirement.

Not all older people fit this new image. But TV and other media now are coming a lot closer to the truth: that the elderly aren't all that different from the rest of Americans. As one retired college professor said in 1982, "Nobody becomes somebody different as they get older."

Moving to the Sunbelt

Shoveling snow, scraping ice off the windshield – that's how many Americans pass the winter. But during the 1970s and 1980s, many Americans decided they were through with winter. As a result, they moved to the warmest parts of the country: the South, Southwest, and West.

During the 1980s, the fastest-growing part of the nation was the Sunbelt. Most of the growth was in California, Arizona, Nevada, New Mexico, Florida, and Texas. In 1991, nearly one out of every eight Americans lived in California. Meanwhile, the cities of the Northeast – called the Rustbelt – lost population or stayed the same.

Americans had been moving to the West and South for decades, but their numbers were greatest during the 1970s and 1980s. People went where the jobs were, and the jobs went where taxes were low. Texas had the oil and aerospace industries, and California had the computer and defense industries. The good weather in these states also attracted many tourists. Some, called "snowbirds," returned to the Sunbelt each winter.

Retired people also moved to the Sunbelt in large numbers. They were looking for a better climate where they could enjoy their new freedom year-round. Retirement communities sprang up throughout the Southwest.

The Sunbelt will continue to grow. Look for Americans to keep moving South and West – as long as they can afford to pay the cost of the air-conditioning. ■

The Sunbelt states, which have the fastest-growing populations in the United States.

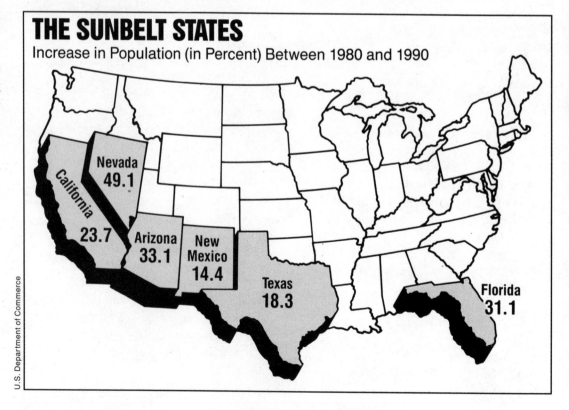

THE SUNBELT STATES
Increase in Population (in Percent) Between 1980 and 1990

Nevada 49.1

California 23.7

Arizona 33.1

New Mexico 14.4

Texas 18.3

Florida 31.1

U.S. Department of Commerce

Years of the Yuppies

She works hard as a stockbroker, sometimes as much as 16 hours a day. She goes to the health club for aerobics and a swim. He is the vice president of a small company and makes calls from his car telephone. Instead of cooking dinner, he usually orders take-out food from restaurants: salmon salads, Szechwan Chinese, or pasta with pesto sauce. Who are they? People of the 1980s and 1990s call them "yuppies."

Yuppies stands for "young urban professionals." These members of the baby boom generation were not born rich, but they are *becoming* rich. They are well educated and have white-collar jobs as, for example, lawyers, bankers, and advertising executives. They are moving up in the world. As a result, they have money, and they spend it – on foreign cars, clothes, eating out (at trendy restaurants), health clubs, Rolex watches. A 1984 study showed that yuppies were three times as likely as other adult Americans to have an American Express card and to travel to foreign countries. They also smoked less and were twice as likely to exercise regularly.

Yuppies want the best for themselves and their children. Their parents had provided nice homes in the suburbs, summers at camp, and the chance to go to college.

But to provide the same things in the 1980s cost a lot more than in the 1950s and 1960s. In those years, only the father usually worked outside the home. In yuppie families, both parents usually work outside the home in order to live as well as their parents had.

Many people see the yuppies as self-centered and interested only in money. Movies like *Wall Street* and *St. Elmo's Fire* showed the bad side of the high-spending, high-debt lifestyle of yuppies. As the 1980s ended – and the economic boom with it – yuppies became more concerned with saving for their children's college education and their own retirement. ■

A young stockbroker and a corporate raider making shady business deals in *Wall Street*, a movie about the greed of the yuppies.

CHANGES ON THE AIR

There was plenty of "the same old stuff" on TV in the late 1970s and the 1980s. You could always find a detective solving mysteries, a police officer chasing criminals, or a cute family at the dinner table.

But there were also TV shows that stood out from the crowd. Some of them changed our ideas about how TV shows could be made. A few even changed the way many of us felt about some important social issues.

"Saturday Night Live" began to change TV comedy.

A New Comedy Generation

In 1975, a show called "Saturday Night Live" ("SNL") changed TV comedy. Most of the writers, directors, and actors were in their 20s—part of the baby boom generation. And "SNL" fast became popular with baby boom TV watchers.

"I just did a show that I would watch if I were the audience," said the show's young creator, Lorne Michaels. "SNL" made fun of world leaders, family life, dating, and celebrities. Comedy sketches featured a "samurai hotel clerk," a bunch of "killer bees," and cast member Dan Ackroyd playing former president Richard Nixon as a hard-to-kill vampire. "Saturday Night Live" launched the careers of some of America's favorite

funny people: Dan Ackroyd, John Belushi, Chevy Chase, Eddie Murphy, Bill Murray, and Gilda Radner. Popular performers also appeared on the show, including Steve Martin, Paul Simon, and James Taylor.

"Soaps" at Night

Cheating husbands and crying wives . . . family feuds and murder trials . . . glitzy clothes and glamorous lifestyles. This was the stuff daytime soap operas were made of in the 1960s and 1970s. But in 1978, a new series called "Dallas" made the biggest news on television. Dallas was a "prime-time" soap opera, shown during the evening.

"Dallas" was the story of an oil-rich Texas family, the Ewings. The Ewing clan was headed by the honest and upright Miss Ellie and her (usually honest) husband, Jock. But TV viewers all knew who really ran the family: eldest son J.R. Ewing, the bad guy with the big smile. J.R. was always at the center of the action. At the end of the 1979-80 season, the country was abuzz with the question "Who shot J.R.?"

Other prime-time TV soaps became popular. "Knots Landing" was about more Ewings. This time, they lived in the sex-and-sin suburbs of California. "Dynasty" followed the fortunes of a rich Colorado family. Members of a California wine-making family were the main characters of "Falcon Crest." And there were plenty more. Americans couldn't watch enough rich

"Dallas" became a popular prime-time soap opera.

folks and their troubles. But the prime-time soaps also reflected America's growing fascination with money and material success in the 1980s.

"Real-Life" Drama

Maybe TV show producers ran out of fresh ideas. Maybe they recognized the dramatic possibilities of real-life news stories. Whatever the reason, in the late 1970s and 1980s, producers began basing made-for-TV movies on news stories. And audiences loved it.

One of the first made-for-TV movies based on a real event was made in 1976. In that year, hijackers took over an airplane at the airport in Entebbe, Uganda. The passengers were rescued in a daring action by Israeli commandos. In December 1976, viewers watched the TV movie *Victory at Entebbe*.

A scene from *The Thorn Birds*, a popular TV miniseries.

The Miniseries

The major TV hits of the 1970s were comedies: "The Mary Tyler Moore Show," "All in the Family," "M*A*S*H," "Happy Days," "Sanford and Son." But at the same time, Americans were also in the mood for hours of television drama . . . as long as somebody called it a "miniseries."

Producer David Wolper worked on some of the most popular miniseries (*Roots, North and South, The Thorn Birds*). He said, "A good miniseries must fulfill [two] categories: One, the book it's based on has to be a big bestseller. . . . Two, the story has to be about a great sociological event—the Holocaust, slavery."

THEN & NOW

Medical dramas have always been popular on TV. In the 1960s, there were "Ben Casey" and "Dr. Kildare." Both were dedicated young doctors who often fought with hospital bosses for the good of their patients. In the 1970s, "Medical Center" starred Chad Everett as a doctor in a medical school setting. "Marcus Welby, M.D." starred grandfatherly Robert Young as a wise family doctor.

All of these shows were known for dealing with "controversial" topics. But the big medical drama of the 1980s, "St. Elsewhere,"

outdid them all. Its story lines included mercy killing, crime, AIDS, mental illness, and rape. It also treated doctors and nurses as humans—people who struggle with family, sexual, and even drug problems.

In the 1990s, a much lighter medical show became popular. "Doogie Howser, M.D." was about a 17-year-old doctor, a young genius who made it through medical school in record time. More than one viewer commented that the idea of a "kid doctor" was hard to believe. But to many, the idea of a 17-year-old who didn't mind being called "Doogie" was even harder to believe.

No TV show hit America as hard as *Roots*. A 1977 miniseries, *Roots* followed black writer Alex Haley's family history before, during, and after slavery. The story followed a young African boy, Kunta Kinte, from his birth to his kidnapping by slave traders in Africa. It then told of his life as a slave in the United States.

For eight nights in January of 1977, millions of Americans were glued to their TV sets. "Out it came," reported *The New Republic*, "the dreadful story [of slavery] which we have spent a century [trying to forget] like a shocking childhood incident. . . . It's good, though, that it's out in the open." Journalists reported that many families began to search for their family roots — by recording the stories of older relatives, for example. Many African-American parents named their new baby boys Kunta Kinte. And *Roots* created a surge of sympathy among America's whites too. "From now on, I will see black through different eyes," a 62-year-old white woman told *Newsweek* magazine. ∎

The miniseries Roots *showed Americans what slavery had been like. It also got many people interested in their family's past. Rent the video, or borrow it from your local public library.*

Make a family tree showing previous generations of your family. Talk to older relatives about their childhood and their parents. How many generations of ancestors can you trace?

If you were a television show producer, what recent news event would you choose for a real-life drama? Who would you cast as the lead actors?

In 1977, the miniseries *Roots* showed Americans what slavery had been like.

Staying Home...for Entertainment!

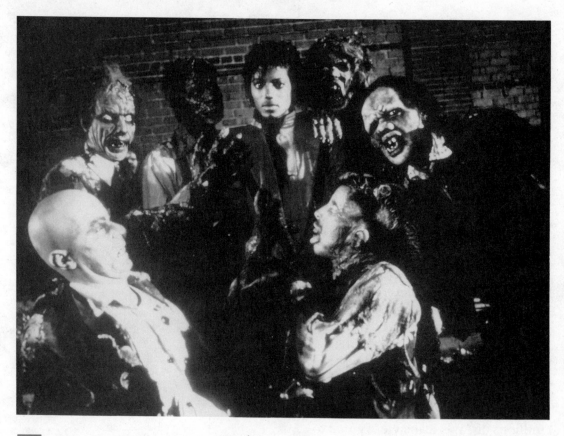

Singer Michael Jackson (top center) in his popular "Thriller" music video. Music videos, made popular by MTV, feature flashy, quick-changing images.

Twenty years ago, who would have thought that you could watch the latest movies right at home . . . on a wide-screen TV. . .whenever you wanted to watch them . . . and with *no* commercials! Who would have thought that you might have 40 or 50 TV channels to choose from?

It's no wonder more and more Americans are staying home for entertainment (with plenty of electronic "toys," of course). These days, a Saturday night date can mean renting a movie from a video store, borrowing it from the library, or tuning it in on a cable TV channel. And

watching movies at home – alone or with friends – is much cheaper than going to the local movie theater.

In fact, some American homes are beginning to look like movie theaters. They have wide-screen TVs, the latest videocassette recorders (VCRs), laser-disk players, and sound systems.

American TV viewers have more choices than ever before. By mid-1989, about 52 million American homes were wired to receive cable TV. More than 60 million households owned a VCR. As a result, viewing habits changed. The three major TV networks (ABC, CBS, and NBC) were losing viewers.

Martha Quinn, a popular "veejay" (host) on MTV.

I Want My MTV

At 12:01 A.M. on August 1, 1981, up to 2.5 million cable subscribers watched as a cartoon rocket went off and a voice said, "Ladies and gentlemen . . . rock and roll!" And with that, MTV—the first around-the-clock all-music TV channel—went on the air.

Throughout the rest of the 1980s, the sound and style of "music videos"—brief performances of hit songs—were everywhere. What was that style? Flashy, quick-changing images. Dancing. Trendy clothes. Sex appeal. And MTV fans couldn't get enough. The MTV style showed up everywhere: on TV commercials (Diet Coke, for example), in the movies (*Flashdance, Top Gun*), even on TV shows ("Miami Vice").

Despite its popularity, MTV has its critics. Some people think the videos are too sexy—or sex*ist*. Women's groups have objected to lyrics and images that portray sexual violence toward women. Religious groups have said that some videos misuse religious images and symbols.

Whether you love it or hate it, MTV is a powerful force in the TV lineup. In fact, it's been around long enough for the creation of a "Classic MTV" show for video "oldies" . . . favorite videos from the early 1980s!

Only 64 percent of the viewers watched the networks on a typical evening. In 1979, the number had been 90 percent.

From network to cable. From 15-minute programs to miniseries. Television has come a long way since the 1950s. It helps us understand history, social problems, and politics. It helps us laugh at ourselves. Young and old, rich and poor, almost all of us watch TV. And because we do, television has become one of the most important forces in American life. ■

HOUSEHOLDS WITH VCRs
(1980-1990, in Millions)

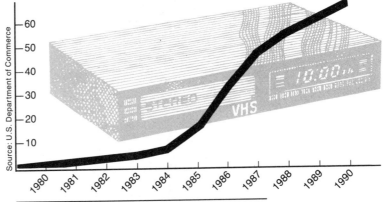

Source: U.S. Department of Commerce

May the Force Be with You . . .

"Pure sweet fun" was what one reviewer called it. The movie was called *Star Wars*. It was a lively, comic-book-style space adventure from a new young moviemaker, George Lucas. *Star Wars* was a surprise to most moviegoers.

The plot was simple. Space rebels (the good guys) were out to keep the evil Galactic Empire (the bad guys) from using a giant space station (the Death Star) to control the whole galaxy. The rebels included a tough-talking princess, a not-too-honest space pilot, and a farm boy (Luke Skywalker) who could call on a mysterious power source known as the Force.

The huge success of *Star Wars* gave George Lucas the money to make two sequels: *The Empire Strikes Back* in 1980 and *Return of the Jedi* in 1983. But it was also a part of an explosion of movies with outer-space plots and lots of special effects: *Close Encounters of the Third Kind, E.T. The Extra-Terrestrial,* plus *Superman, Star Trek,* and their sequels. And when President Ronald Reagan proposed a new weapons system as a shield against nuclear attack, he called it "Star Wars"! ■

A scene from *Star Wars*, the surprise blockbuster movie of 1977.

New Voices

"**I** am . . . exploring the oppressions, the insanities, the loyalties, and the triumphs of black women," said black writer Alice Walker in the 1970s. Walker's 1982 novel *The Color Purple* won both the Pulitzer Prize and the National Book Award. Later, it was made into a movie starring Whoopi Goldberg, Oprah Winfrey, and Danny Glover. Walker's success was echoed by several other new voices—successful black women writers of the 1970s and 1980s.

The time was right for the new writers. Americans were ready to listen. The women's liberation ("women's lib") movement of the late 1960s and the 1970s helped Americans take female writers more seriously. And the civil rights movement of the 1950s and 1960s had focused attention on the problems of racism and sexism in the United States. As a result, both black and white readers were ready to hear the voices of black women writers.

In 1983, Gloria Naylor's *The Women of Brewster Place* won the American Book Award. This novel contained stories about the lives of several black women. The stories also came alive in a TV miniseries starring Cicely Tyson, Paul Winfield, and Oprah Winfrey.

Other successful new voices were Toni Morrison (*Song of Solomon, Beloved, Tar Baby*), Maya Angelou (*I Know Why the Caged Bird Sings, Singin' and Swingin' and Gettin' Merry Like Christmas*), Nikki Giovanni (*Gemini* and several books of poetry), Ntozake Shange (the play "For Colored Girls Who Have Considered Suicide/When the Rainbow Is Enuf"), and Alice Childress (*A Hero Ain't Nothing but a*

Writers Alice Walker (top) and Toni Morrison (bottom).

Sandwich and *Rainbow Jordan*). Writer Toni Morrison's novel *Beloved* won the Pulitzer Prize in 1988. She once wrote about the special task of the "black" novel: "It should be beautiful, and powerful, but it should also *work*. It should have something in it that . . . opens the door and points the way. . . that suggests what the conflicts are, what the problems are. But it need not solve those problems. . . ."

Writers like Morrison may not believe they have to solve America's racial problems. But their writings give all Americans a clearer, more powerful understanding of what it means to be an African-American . . . and a woman. ■

Those Supermarket Tabloids

Sexy lawyer dumps hubby and career — to marry a killer!

Famous movie star tells all . . . rock sensation marries his mistress . . . talk-show host threatens to quit. . . . In the 1970s and 1980s, there was a boom in gossip—gossip about celebrities, politicians, and ordinary Americans who, for a short time, became famous.

Celebrity gossip was nothing new. In the 1930s and 1940s, New York newspaper writer Walter Winchell's gossip column was very powerful. Movie stars, politicians, nightclub owners, and millionaires all wanted to stay on Winchell's good side so he would write good things about them.

But never before had gossip been such good business. In the 1970s, the gossipy magazine *People* became one of the most successful magazines in years. Other magazines followed the same format. And in the 1980s, celebrity stories were the center of two hit TV shows, "Lifestyles of the Rich and Famous" and "Entertainment Tonight."

Many Americans got their weekly dose of gossip from tabloid newspapers sold at supermarket checkout stands. The *National Enquirer* and the *Star*

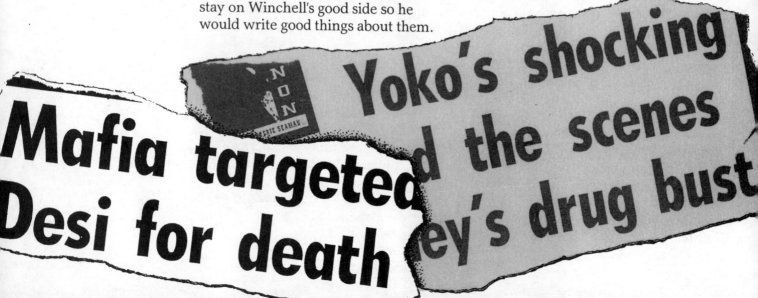

Mafia targeted Desi for death

Yoko's shocking ... the scenes

...ey's drug bust

Madonna's s[...]
days — eating ou[...]
cans and posing in the nude

thing to get there. And [...]

SECRET EVIDENCE
REVEALS SHOCKIN[...]
TRUTH AT LAST

Charles mo[...]
with Di afte[...]
save their c[...]

were the most famous of these. They reported all kinds of sensational "news"—from celebrity scandals to space alien visits.

True or *Not* True?

Do Americans believe the stories they read in tabloids? Some people read them as a joke. But many people believe they are true. Some celebrities, including actor Carol Burnett, have taken tabloid publishers to court for writing lies about them.

Is today's gossip different from the celebrity stories of 50 years ago? Yes, says writer Nicholas Lemann.

"[Celebrities] aren't any longer people we think of as our betters—they're what we would be ourselves, if only we could lose fifteen pounds and get a promotion." In other words, he says, we like to know that stars are "just folks" like us—folks who have problems with their marriages, their children, with drinking, weight, careers, and so on. ∎

Have you ever bought a tabloid because of a "spicy" headline, only to find that the story did not live up to its promise? How did you feel about it? Would you call this "false advertising"? Describe your experience.

They reported all kinds of sensational "news" — from celebrity scandals to space alien visits.

From Disco to Rap

In 1975, "The Hustle" hit the airwaves. And Americans hustled — wearing the polyester jumpsuits, platform heels, and long hair popular at the time. Under the mirrored balls and strobe lights at the local dance hall, Americans took up the complicated new style of dancing known as *disco*.

Saturday Night Fever, a hit movie of 1977, helped spread the disco craze. In the movie, young people find romance and excitement inside the local disco (officially called a *discotheque*). The movie was a blockbuster. For the first time in a generation, Americans went back into the dance studios. They were eager to learn the complicated steps of the samba, the swing, the merengue, and, of course, the hustle.

Yo! Rap Music

But the smooth sound of disco wasn't "fresh" enough for many young blacks. While dancers were discoing in other parts of New York City, disc jockeys in black dance clubs were trying something new. They used their turntables to mix instrumental bits from different songs. And while the music played, an MC, or rapper, would chant (or "rap") a rhyming lyric to go with the music.

Soon, young black performers took up the new sound. During the last half of the 1980s, rap turned up in commercials and in many movies. As just one example, filmmaker Spike Lee wanted a "defiant . . . angry. . . rhythmic" song to go with the riot scenes in *Do the Right Thing*. To get that sound, he turned to the rap group Public Enemy.

Rappers soon became famous. Pepsi-Cola hired rapper [M. C.] Hammer to sell the soft drink in TV commercials. Rap star Will Smith made it to prime-

Stars of the disco era: actor John Travolta (left) in *Saturday Night Fever* and singer Donna Summer (right).

time TV with a sitcom, "The Fresh Prince of Bel-Air." But rap (or "hip-hop," as fans call it) is still about lives of young urban African-Americans. Rappers sing about street violence, drugs, poverty, politics, and sex.

"[T]his music from the streets and ghettos of America makes many people uncomfortable. That's what it's supposed to do," writes Barbara Dority of the Washington Coalition Against Censorship. But many people have objected to the words of some songs. They say rap often shows prejudice against nonblacks. Women's groups say many rap songs put down women with lyrics about sex, anger, and violence.

On the other hand, many rap performers try to be positive role models for their young fans. And rap, like rock 'n' roll, gives a voice to Americans who sometimes feel they are not heard. ■

In 1990, members of rap group 2 Live Crew were arrested because a judge had ruled their songs were obscene. Other rap groups have been criticized for their lyrics. What do you think of attempts to ban certain rap songs? Do you think that an album some consider obscene should be pulled from music stores? Why or why not?

Break Dancing

Poppin'... lockin'... the head spin ... the wave ... the back spin ... these moves are part of a modern-day dance style known as *break dancing*. Born in New York's South Bronx in the late 1970s, break dancing developed as part of the hip-hop, or rap, music trend. It was the dance of the young and street smart. "The dancers started breaking 'cause it was symbolic of the streets," said one New York breaker.

Soon, movies such as *Breakin'* and *Beat Street* spread the break-dance trend across the country. People could learn the moves by renting how-to videos. The publicity bothered some breakers. "Now that breaking is being commercialized, it can't be the same because it doesn't have the heart," said a member of the Big Apple Breakers.

Rap stars Hammer (left), and Will Smith of "The Fresh Prince of Bel- Air" (right).

Olympic No-Show

"**I**'m disappointed, *every* athlete in America is disappointed. But I hope that in some way our sacrifice will keep the planet Earth peaceful," said Edwin Moses before the 1980 summer Olympics in Moscow.

Moses, the top 400-meter hurdler in the world, did not compete at the 1980 Olympics in Moscow. No American athlete did.

A President's Decision

In 1979, the Soviet Union invaded Afghanistan and took over its government. The United States opposed the invasion. To express this protest, President Jimmy Carter organized a boycott of the 1980 Olympic Games held in the Soviet Union's capital. Eventually, more than 50 nations joined the U.S. boycott.

Carter's decision angered many American athletes who had spent years training for the Olympics. The boycott shattered their dreams.

"I think President Carter's decision to boycott the 1980 Games was a mistake,

President Carter (above left) with the 1980 U.S. Olympic team during ceremonies at the Capitol. The United States boycotted the summer Olympics in Moscow (right).

themselves were joyless," wrote Lord Killanin, president of the International Olympic Committee from 1972 to 1980. "Too often we were thinking of the missing people, wondering and weighing up what might have happened." ■

Often, the Olympic Games are affected by political issues. The cold war rivalries of the 1950s and the boycotts of the 1980s are examples of this.

Do you agree with President Carter's decision to boycott the 1980 Olympics?

Do you think the Olympics will ever be free of political issues? Why or why not?

Miruts Yifter (left) of Ethiopia won the 5,000- and 10,000-meter runs. Britain's Sebastian Coe (below) winning the 1,500-meter run.

but when the athletes complained, they were made to appear as unpatriotic, bickering, young brats," said sprinter Carl Lewis.

Thrilling Performances

Although only 81 nations competed in the 1980 summer Olympics, there were many exciting performances.

British milers Steve Ovett and Sebastian Coe raced against each other in two events. The first was the 800-meter run. Coe, the world record holder, was expected to win. But in the race, Coe fell behind early and was unable to catch up. Ovett won; Coe finished second. Coe couldn't believe he had lost. "I felt empty," he said, "and I had just wasted eleven years' work."

But Coe had another chance at Olympic gold—the 1,500-meter run. This time it was Coe's turn to surprise the world. Ovett was favored to win, but Coe was the victor.

A 36-year-old Ethiopian, Miruts Yifter, came out on top in both the 5,000 and 10,000 meters. Yifter had won a bronze medal in the 1972 games.

Although the athletes performed very well, the 1980 Olympics were a disappointment. "The Games

The Era of the NBA

In 1965, pro basketball teams played before few fans, were rarely seen on television, and represented only nine cities. Twenty-five years later, more than 17 million fans attended games, television networks paid tens of millions of dollars to broadcast games, and the NBA was made up of 27 teams across the country.

Basketball superstars Moses Malone (left) and Larry Bird (right).

Growing Up – and Out

In 1965, team owners did not know whether pro basketball would be popular outside the nine cities with teams. The owners wondered if there were enough good players for more teams. But in the late 1960s, the NBA took a deep breath and added five new teams over the next three years.

In 1967, a rival league called the American Basketball Association (ABA) was founded. The ABA began with 11 teams and lasted until 1976. When the ABA came to an end, four of its top teams joined the NBA: the Denver Nuggets, Indiana Pacers, San Antonio Spurs, and New York Nets.

Four more teams were added to the NBA in the late 1980s: the Minnesota Timberwolves, Charlotte Hornets, Orlando Magic, and Miami Heat.

Frustration and Success

Like most expansion clubs, these four new teams played terribly during their first seasons. "The toughest thing

Air Jordan: Basketball's Best

Michael Jordan makes basketball look easy. He executes stunning slam dunks, plays tough defense, and makes spectacular passes to his teammates.

Jordan, a guard for the Chicago Bulls, led the league in scoring for five straight years, from 1987 to 1991. He was the NBA's rookie of the year in 1985 and most valuable player in 1988 and 1991. He led the Bulls to their first-ever NBA championship in 1991.

"There's nothing you can do against him except work, hope, and pray," said Coach Chuck Daly of the Detroit Pistons.

Basketball fans loved to watch the superstar. The Bulls' average attendance increased from 6,000 in the 1983–1984 season to 18,000 in 1990–1991. The Bulls sold out 181 straight games.

Jordan has appeared in commercials for Nike, Coca-Cola, McDonald's, Wheaties, Chevrolet, and many other companies. In one year, Nike earned more than $100 million on its Air Jordan gym shoe. McDonald's even named a sandwich after him – the McJordan.

In the early 1990s, Jordan earned $10 million to $15 million a year from endorsements and investments. He earned another $3 million playing basketball.

Michael Jordan (left). "There's nothing you can do against him except work, hope, and pray," said a rival team's coach.

was trying to maintain a positive attitude to keep on going. Even though you are an expansion team, you never envision losing 17 in a row at the start," said coach Ron Rothstein of the Heat.

Despite all the losses, the new teams were popular. The Charlotte Hornets led the NBA in attendance in their first season. They were the first expansion team to do so. "I dreamed of sellouts before we ever got our ballclub," said Hornets owner George Shinn. The next year, the Minnesota Timberwolves broke the Hornets' record when more than 1 million fans attended their games during their first season.

Between 1983 and 1990, total attendance at NBA games increased by 80 percent, from 9 million to 17 million. The four newest expansion clubs contributed more than 3 million fans. As the NBA entered the 1990s, it was truly a *national* league – and bigger than ever. ■

SUPER BOWL SUPERPOWERS

Three football "dynasties" ruled professional football in the mid-1970s and 1980s. In pro football, a dynasty is a team that wins more than one Super Bowl within a few years. And the dynasties in those years were something to see.

The Steelers and the Cowboys

The Pittsburgh Steelers and the Dallas Cowboys met in the January 1976 Super Bowl. Both teams came into the game having already won a 1970s championship.

Dallas played a new style of football; its "shotgun" offense caught the

Pittsburgh Steelers' Lynn Swann making a diving catch in the 1976 Super Bowl.

Cowboys' opponents off their guard. Pittsburgh played old-fashioned football; the Steelers' "steel curtain" defense overpowered their opponents. As tackle "Mean" Joe Greene is quoted in the book *The Super Bowl*, "We would look at each other and we knew. We simply weren't going to lose."

The teams agreed on one thing, though. They hated each other. "Yeah, we disliked them," said the Cowboys' Cliff Harris. "The rough, rugged, basic Steelers . . . the clean, cosmopolitan, finesse Cowboys . . . . That contrast . . . that was the thing between us."

The 1976 game was a Super Bowl classic. Dallas led at halftime, but the Steelers broke open a 21–10 lead in the final quarter. Dallas came back, but the Steel Curtain prevailed, 21–17.

For the Cowboys, the loss was

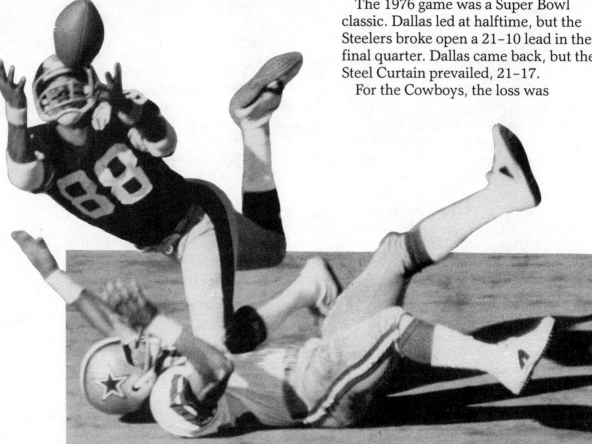

heartbreaking. But Dallas fans had plenty to smile about in the 1970s. The Cowboys played in five Super Bowls that decade, winning two. By the 1977–1978 season, they were known as "America's team." That year, they played the Denver Broncos for the championship. With their star quarterback Roger Staubach and their "doomsday" defense, the Cowboys beat the Broncos 27–10.

The Cowboys did not reign as America's team for long, though. One year after Dallas triumphed over Denver, Pittsburgh returned to the Super Bowl for a rematch with the Cowboys. The game was a wild shoot-out between two of the greatest quarterbacks in the league: Roger Staubach of the Cowboys and Terry Bradshaw of the Steelers.

With six minutes left in the game, Pittsburgh seemed to have it easily won. Bradshaw's four touchdown passes had helped the Steelers build a 35–17 lead. Then Staubach rallied the Cowboys, throwing two TD passes. But the Steelers held on to win 35–31.

One year later, in 1980, Pittsburgh made history. The Steelers beat the Los Angeles Rams for the championship, their fourth Super Bowl victory in only six years.

Joe Montana and the 49ers

Pittsburgh and Dallas had great quarterbacks, but the San Francisco 49ers were led by perhaps the greatest of all: Joe Montana. The 49ers dominated the 1980s by winning four Super Bowls.

The 49ers won their first Super Bowl in 1982. "We were so young, we didn't know we weren't supposed to win . . . ," said former 49ers guard Randy Cross. "We were just naive enough to think that anything was possible, even a Super Bowl."

The young 49ers shocked the Cincinnati Bengals 26–21 in Super Bowl XVI in 1982. The 49ers would go on to win Super Bowls in 1985, 1989, and 1990.

By the 1989 season, the 49ers were known as the "team of the '80s." They stormed through the playoffs that year, dominating their opponents. When the Denver Broncos prepared to play them in Super Bowl XXIV, no one gave the Broncos a chance. Once the game started, neither did the 49ers. Scoring eight touchdowns in their first 11 possessions, San Francisco embarrassed Denver. Montana broke Terry Bradshaw's Super Bowl record by throwing five touchdown passes. The game's final score was the most lopsided in Super Bowl history: 55–10. ■

San Francisco 49ers quarterback Joe Montana.

What pro football team appears to be the team of the 1990s? Are there any new dynasties in the making?

Women's Surge in Sports

Martina Navratilova (left) and Chris Evert (right).

In the 1970s and 1980s, women's sports became a big business, and female athletes thrilled millions. They gained large television audiences and endorsed products. Especially in tennis and track, women led the way.

Tennis Greats

In tennis, two women dominated: Chris Evert and Martina Navratilova.

Evert was a teenage sensation. She began playing professionally in 1972 at the age of 18. By 1990, she had won

Wimbledon three times and been U.S. singles champ six times.

Navratilova grew up in Czechoslovakia but moved to the United States in 1975. Her quickness, strong first serve, and aggressive style of play made her the top female player in the world. She won 15 major tournaments during the 1980s. By 1989, she had won more than $15 million as a professional.

Olympic Stars

"It was a 20-year dream. At that moment I knew everything was worth it. I felt so happy inside that I had it won I just had to let it out," said Florence Griffith Joyner in 1988. Griffith Joyner had just won an Olympic gold medal in the 100-meter run at Seoul, South Korea.

"Flo Jo" became one of the world's best-known female athletes. Her running ability impressed sports fans, and her unique running outfits captured everyone's attention. Griffith Joyner wore flashy one-legged bodysuits and decals on her long fingernails.

Flo Jo's sister-in-law, Jackie Joyner-Kersee, won the heptathlon and long jump at the 1988 summer Olympics. Four years earlier, at the Los Angeles Olympics, Joyner-Kersee had missed winning the heptathlon by five points. "I always think about 1984," said Joyner-Kersee. "So many people gave me so much support after *not* winning, I wanted to give something back." ■

Why do you think women's sports became a big business in the 1970s and 1980s? What changing attitudes toward women may have played a part?

Jackie Joyner-Kersee (left) competing in the 55-meter hurdles. Florence Griffith Joyner (right) receiving the Jesse Owens International Trophy in 1989.

Baseball: The Salary Explosion

Imagine working for seven months each year, traveling across the United States playing baseball, and earning $800,000. This is the life of the average major-league baseball player.

In 1980, outfielder Dave Winfield was the first player to earn $1 million. The deal made headlines.

"When salaries got to one million dollars, I said that was the top," said Toronto Blue Jays president Paul Beeston in 1989. "Then it hit two million. Now, who knows?" The answer came soon: by 1991, 32 players were making more than $3 million a year.

The Reserve Clause

Before 1975, baseball players lacked bargaining power. The reserve clause made the team owners very powerful. This rule, adopted in 1880, gave teams the right to keep players until they retired. Other teams could not obtain these players except in a trade. Players fought the rule in court. In a 1975

The Toronto SkyDome, the luxurious home of the Toronto Blue Jays, drew a record 4 million fans in 1991.

ruling on a case involving players Dave McNally and Andy Messersmith, an arbitrator threw out the reserve clause. Players and owners then agreed to a new rule.

Today, major leaguers who play for six years can become free agents. Free agents can join the team that offers the most money.

The New Numbers

In February of 1989, Boston Red Sox pitcher Roger Clemens signed a contract worth $2.5 million a year for three years, making him the highest-paid player in baseball. Ten months later, the Minnesota Twins' Kirby Puckett broke the $3 million mark and became the highest-paid player—but not for long.

As one writer noted, "The time has come when utility infielders drive Rolls-Royces and the superstars fly in private jets."

Many people think it is ridiculous that ballplayers make so much money. But others point out that because of the players, America spends millions of dollars to watch baseball. Fans pay for tickets to the games. TV networks pay for the right to broadcast games. In 1990, CBS and ESPN paid more than $16 million to each team. Local TV and radio stations pay too. Supporters of the high salaries argue that since the players are bringing in all this money, they deserve to take some of it home. And as long as the money is there, who can blame the players for taking it? ■

Do you think sports superstars like Kirby Puckett and Michael Jordan deserve the millions of dollars they are paid? What do you think of athletes who hold out before signing contracts until they are paid more money? Are they being greedy, or are they simply demanding fair pay?

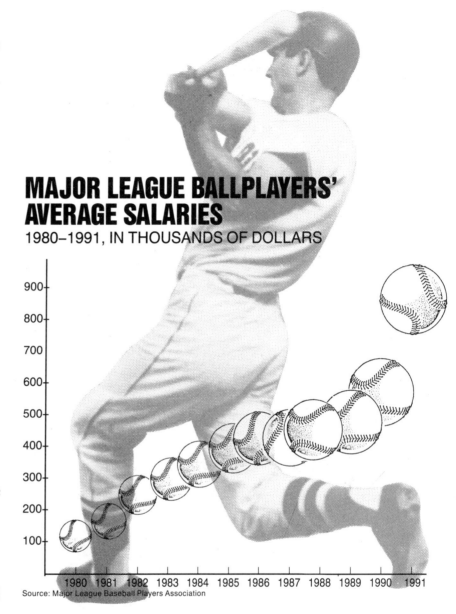

MAJOR LEAGUE BALLPLAYERS' AVERAGE SALARIES
1980–1991, IN THOUSANDS OF DOLLARS

Source: Major League Baseball Players Association

THEN & NOW

As the graph shows, the average salary for baseball players has skyrocketed. It increased six-fold between 1980 and 1990. Some experts think the *average* salary will be $1 million a year before the mid-1990s.

They Didn't Play by the Rules

"**I**'d like to say my name is Benjamin Sinclair Johnson, Jr., and this world record will last 50 years, maybe 100," said Ben Johnson in 1988.

Johnson, a Canadian runner, had just won the 100-meter dash at the Olympic Games in Seoul, South Korea. He broke the world record with a time of 9.79 seconds. But the next day, Johnson's gold medal and world record were taken away from him by Olympic officials. Johnson also was suspended from all international meets for the next two years.

Johnson had been found guilty of using a steroid, a dangerous kind of drug that helps build muscle fibers. Olympic rules forbid the use of steroids.

Unfortunately, Ben Johnson's case is not unique. Drugs and gambling also hurt many pro sports in the 1980s.

The Drug Plague

A noted sports medicine specialist has stated, "I have encountered very few sports which have not been affected in one way or another by doping."

Canadian sprinter Ben Johnson competing (left) and testifying (right) about his use of steroids.

Baseball's Pete Rose (left) was banned from the game for life for gambling. Football player Chuck Muncie (right) leaving the Miami Dolphins training camp after failing a drug test.

In 1989, illegal sales of steroids in the United States were estimated to have totaled $100 million.

In response to the growing drug problem, the NFL began testing all players for drugs in 1986. Players are tested for such drugs as marijuana, cocaine, and steroids. Tests have found that, unfortunately, a number of these pros have used drugs.

"The more we learn about the drug problem, the more we realize how bad it is," said former NFL commissioner Pete Rozelle.

The Curse of Gambling

Baseball has also had its share of drug problems. But in the 1980s, the biggest baseball scandal had to do with gambling. In 1989, Pete Rose, baseball's all-time hits leader, was banned from the game for life by Commissioner Bart Giamatti.

Rose was accused of betting on baseball games—even those involving his own team. An attorney hired by the commissioner prepared a 225-page report on Rose's wrongdoings. Rose and his lawyers fought the charges. Finally, in August 1989, Rose saw that he could not win that bet. He agreed to the lifetime ban.

"The matter of Mr. Rose is now closed," said Giamatti. "Let no one think that it did not hurt baseball . . . . Let it also be clear that no individual is superior to the game." ■

In 1991, baseball's Hall of Fame directors ruled that no players banned from baseball could be selected for the hall. So Pete Rose will never get that honor—even though, on the field, he was surely one of the game's greatest players. The decision set off a big debate among baseball fans. How do you feel about it? Should Rose have a chance to be selected? Or should he be kept out because of his off-the-field problems?

Because of the widespread use of steroids and other drugs, most sports now require athletes to be tested for drugs. Some people say that this invades athletes' privacy or that it treats them like criminals. Do you agree? If so, how do you think sports teams should deal with their drug problems?

Do you think drug testing should be required for other professions? Why or why not? If you do think so, which professionals should have to be tested?

REAGANOMICS

One reason Ronald Reagan was elected president in 1980 was that he promised to improve the economy. During most of the 1970s, the United States had suffered from "stagflation," a combination of inflation and recession. That is, prices were rising, but business activity was decreasing. By late 1980, prices were rising more than 13 percent a year. At the same time, about one out of 14 workers was unemployed.

Reagan's ideas for improving the economy were known as *supply-side economics*. Most people, though, called them *Reaganomics*.

Reaganomics proposed to improve the economy by reducing personal and business taxes. Tax cuts would give people and businesses more money to save and to spend. Businesses could invest in better equipment and increase production. More production would lead to more jobs. And more jobs would mean more people paying taxes. That way, the government would not lose any income, even though it cut taxes.

"If we cut tax rates deeply and permanently, we'll be removing many of the barriers that hold everyone back. Those who have the least will gain the most, " one Reagan campaign commercial promised. After Reagan was elected, he asked Congress to cut personal income taxes by 25 percent over a three-year period. It was the biggest tax cut in U.S. history.

Less Government

In addition to lower taxes, Reagan proposed that the federal government give more power to the state governments. This program, called New Federalism, reduced Washington's control over the states. It also withdrew federal money that had gone to state governments. As a result, states had more responsibility but less money to work with. Many states raised taxes to make up for the money lost.

Reaganomics also aimed to cut spending for federal programs. The administration fired workers in many government departments, such as the departments of Health and Human Services and of Housing and Urban Development. It also cut spending on domestic programs. Funds were reduced for programs in the areas of education, environmental protection, food stamps, job training, and public housing.

Merger Mania

It was the biggest business merger in U.S. history. On November 30, 1988, the food and tobacco firm RJR Nabisco was sold for more than $25 billion. The buyers were members of the investment firm Kohlberg, Kravis, Roberts, and Co.

The takeover of RJR Nabisco was only one of many such deals. Hundreds of business firms were bought by other firms during the 1980s. And many different industries were involved in these takeovers. For example, in the early 1980s, Du Pont bought Conoco Oil, and Sears, Roebuck & Co. bought Dean Witter Reynolds. Santa Fe Industries became the owner of Southern Pacific. In 1984, Chevron took over Gulf Oil, and Texaco took over Getty Oil. In 1985, tobacco company Philip Morris acquired General Foods. In 1988, Philip Morris grew still bigger by buying Kraft Foods.

These big mergers worried many economists. In many mergers, the buyer often paid only part of the purchase price in cash and borrowed the rest. As a result,

many American companies owed huge amounts of money. Economists worried that if the economy took a downturn, companies with large debts might be unable to make their interest payments—and be forced to close their doors.

A display of the products of RJR Nabisco at the time it was sold to an investment firm.

In addition, the Reagan administration increased military spending. Between 1981 and 1984, the defense budget rose from $135 billion to $231 billion. With less money coming in, and more money being spent, the United States increased its huge budget deficit. The national debt skyrocketed. By 1989, after Reagan's eight years in office, the United States owed about $2.8 trillion. More than $240 billion a year – or about $660 million each day – went to pay interest on money the government had borrowed.

Reaganomics also helped continue a trend that had begun in the 1970s: the rich were getting richer while everyone else was getting poorer. From 1977 to 1991, the income of the richest fifth of U.S. families – adjusted for inflation – rose 29 percent. The income of the second fifth rose by 2 percent. The income of the other three-fifths *fell*. The hardest hit was the poorest fifth, which suffered a drop in income of 13.2 percent. The top 1 percent of American families earned more than

Effects on the Nation

What were the results of Reaganomics?

On the plus side, there was a sharp drop in the inflation rate. From a high of nearly 13 percent in 1980, the rate fell to less than 2 percent in 1986. By 1990, the rate of inflation was up to 6.1 percent. But "double-digit" inflation seemed to be a thing of the past.

On the minus side, many individuals were hit hard by Reaganomics. Although income taxes were cut, other taxes – especially Social Security taxes – were raised. And cuts in domestic programs hurt America's poor and middle-class citizens. To make matters worse, in 1981 the United States suffered a serious economic downturn. About one out of 13 workers was unemployed. As a result, the government's income from taxes went down, and it could not cover its expenses. To make up the difference, it borrowed money.

INFLATION RATES
1980–1990

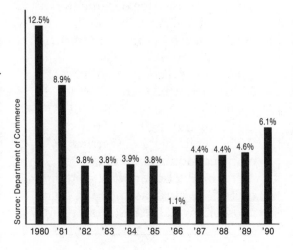

the bottom 40 percent of families put together. Those who suffered the most under Reaganomics were minorities and one-parent families, especially those headed by women. ■

Ask several people you know these two questions:

How did Reaganomics affect the country?

How did it affect you?

Write a paragraph comparing the answers you get.

The stealth fighter, designed to be nearly invisible to radar, was part of President Reagan's buildup of American military strength.

THEN & NOW

In 1791, the federal government owed more than $75 million. Two hundred years later, in 1991, the federal government owed more than $3 trillion. The four biggest increases in the national debt took place during our three biggest wars and during the Reagan years. The debt jumped in 1862 through 1865 – years of the Civil War. It jumped again in 1918 and 1919 – during and just after World War I. The debt increased sharply in 1942 through 1945 – World War II. The largest dollar amount increase, however, took place between 1980 and 1988. During the Reagan years, the U.S. government piled up more than twice as much debt as it had in its entire history. And it is continuing to spend more than it takes in.

Troubled Thrifts

Workers in Denver taking down the sign outside Silverado Banking, a large savings and loan that went bankrupt in 1989.

In 1989, President George Bush signed into law the Financial Institutions Reform, Recovery, and Enforcement Act. The goal of this act was to solve problems in the nation's troubled thrift (savings and loan, or S&L) industry. The industry was losing thousands of dollars each day. Experts say that ending the crisis will cost more than $500 billion—about $5,000 for every household in America. How did the situation get so out of hand?

The ABCs of S&Ls

To understand how the crisis came about, you need to know what S&Ls are and how they earn profits. *S&Ls* are businesses that specialize in offering savings accounts and home loans. To attract savers, S&Ls pay interest on money in savers' accounts. From the point of view of S&Ls, interest is the cost of getting savers to put money in their accounts. What do S&Ls do with savers' funds? For the most part, they invest them in home loans. Borrowers pay back their loans plus interest—a charge for the use of the loan. S&Ls earn profits when the amount of interest they take in on home loans is greater than the amount of interest they pay out on savings accounts.

For many years, this system worked well. Most S&Ls earned profits, and the industry played an important role in helping people buy homes. But during the late 1970s, a time of high inflation, the S&L industry began to have money problems.

S&Ls Lose Savers

New investments, such as money market funds, were coming on the financial scene. These investments could pay more than twice as much interest as S&L accounts. S&Ls couldn't raise their rates to match these investments, because the government had put a limit on the rates S&Ls could pay. The limit was meant to keep down the cost of home loans. The less interest S&Ls have to pay to savers, the less interest they have to charge borrowers. But the limit also had the unexpected side effect of making the S&L industry less competitive. People began taking their money out of S&Ls and putting it into money market funds and other investments. S&Ls began losing business.

The Government Deregulates

During the late 1970s, both S&Ls and banks pressured the government to deregulate their industries—to do away with some of the rules

that limit what these businesses can and can't do. They wanted the right to decide for themselves what interest rates to offer on their accounts. The S&L industry also wanted the right to make other kinds of loans. The industry believed that it could better compete with banks if it could make various kinds of business loans. Though these loans are riskier than home loans, they can also be more profitable.

In the early 1980s, Congress took steps to deregulate S&Ls and banks. The interest rate limit was taken off most accounts. S&Ls were allowed to offer credit cards and other kinds of consumer loans. S&Ls also were given new powers to invest in business, real estate, and construction loans. Deregulation brought new hope to the industry. But hope soon gave way to headaches.

New Problems Arise

Removing the limit on interest rates turned out to be a mixed blessing. On the one hand, S&Ls were able to win back savers by paying higher rates of interest on accounts. On the other hand, inflation was pushing rates higher and higher. Rates climbed to more than 15 percent. At the same time, S&Ls were collecting much lower rates of interest, such as 4 and 5 percent, on home loans they had made years earlier. Many S&Ls found themselves paying out more in interest than they were taking in.

71 Ohio Savings Institutions Shut For 3 Days in Effort to...

Savings Institution Milked By Its Chief, Regulators Say

Expe... Express Pessimism On Savings Industry's Future

U.S. Has Trouble Coping With Its Savings Empire

Some S&Ls got into deeper trouble when they began to make new kinds of loans. Though they had years of experience in making home loans, they did not have the same kind of know-how when it came to business, consumer, and development loans. Inexperience and poor judgment led some S&Ls to make loans that borrowers could not repay.

Other S&Ls lost money on real estate deals in Texas and other southwestern states. In the early 1980s, the demand for oil was high. So was the price. The oil boom brought more businesses, jobs, and workers to the Southwest. As a result, developers were looking for money to build new office buildings, shopping centers, hotels, and other commercial developments. Some S&Ls saw the oil boom as a golden opportunity to invest in real estate.

When the oil boom went bust in the mid-1980s, these S&Ls lost out twice. Borrowers were unable to repay their loans, and S&Ls had to try to sell their commercial developments at a time when there were very few buyers. In the meantime, the S&Ls had to pay for upkeep on the properties.

Deregulation had also brought out the worst in some industry insiders and newcomers. A few lent money to family and friends for projects that weren't financially sound. Some also used money from their S&Ls to buy themselves expensive cars, homes, and vacations.

In 1987, the S&L industry lost $6 billion. The next year, it lost $11 billion. In 1989, it lost $20 billion. Almost 500 of the nation's 3,200 S&Ls went bankrupt. Another 500 or so were on the edge of bankruptcy. The government body in charge of S&L deposit insurance was in the same condition. When government-insured S&Ls go bankrupt, the government covers the money in accounts so that customers do not lose their savings. At the end of 1988, the Federal Savings and Loan Insurance Corporation (FSLIC) had only $1 billion to cover more than $1 trillion in insured accounts. Something had to be done. In 1989, Congress stepped in with the Financial Institutions Reform, Recovery, and Enforcement Act (FIRREA).

After FIRREA

FIRREA brought sweeping changes to the S&L industry. It required S&Ls to once again specialize in making home loans. It set up the Resolution Trust Corporation (RTC) to manage and sell bankrupt S&Ls. It did away with the FSLIC and set up a new insuring body – the Savings Association Insurance Fund (SAIF). SAIF answers to the Federal Deposit Insurance Corporation (FDIC), the government body that oversees commercial bank deposits. Under FIRREA, S&Ls must pay more for deposit insurance than they paid in the past.

FIRREA also raised reserve and capital requirements for S&Ls. *Reserves* are the amount of money S&Ls must

set aside to cover financial losses. *Capital* is the amount of assets, or worth, an S&L must have to be called financially sound.

The S&L crisis was one of the most serious financial difficulties the United States ever faced. Americans demanded greater financial responsibility from the S&L industry – and hoped that FIRREA would prevent future crises. ∎

President Bush (above) signing a 1989 law to reform the S&L industry. Below, Charles Keating being sworn in at a congressional hearing. Keating, an S&L owner, was arrested for dishonest practices.

Hunger in America

A Salvation Army worker serving meals to homeless people in Pittsburgh.

"**O**ne out of every eight children in the United States – about 5.5 million kids under age 12 – does not get enough to eat," reported the *Chicago Tribune* in 1991. Many adults are going hungry too. In fact, about 20 million Americans are not getting enough to eat.

Low Income

One reason for hunger in America is poverty. Millions of American families have yearly incomes that fall below the poverty line – the minimum amount the government says a family needs to buy food, clothing, and shelter. In 1990, the poverty level for a family of four was $12,700.

A 1991 study done by the Food Research and Action Center found that families whose children were going hungry had incomes 25 percent below the poverty level. These families spent up to one-third of their income on food. However, that added up to only 68 cents per person for each meal.

Government Policies

The U.S. government provides some aid for families needing food. Families whose income falls below a certain level are eligible for food stamps and free school lunches. Low-income mothers and their babies can qualify for food vouchers under the WIC (Supplemental Feeding Program for Women, Infants, and Children). These programs can help needy families get at least some of the food they need.

However, government food programs do not reach everyone who needs help. For instance, only two-thirds of those eligible for food stamps in 1986 actually received the stamps. Why? One reason is that changes in government rules caused much disorder in the system. In addition, many who are eligible for food stamps never apply for them. "Don't ask me to apply for food stamps," said one man

LIVING BELOW THE POVERTY LINE

Percentage of Population

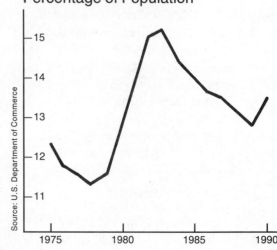

Source: U.S. Department of Commerce

in need. "I just won't go through that."

Americans going hungry is more than a national shame. One doctors' group called hunger in America "a national health epidemic." ■

You are in charge: the president has appointed you to solve the problem of hunger in the United States. What would you do? What could the government and private citizens do? Write up a series of ideas that you think would start solving the problem.

One of New York City's homeless people sleeping on a sidewalk.

Homelessness in America

In the 1980s, Americans became used to a painful sight. They saw people sleeping in cardboard boxes and old cars and on sidewalks, park benches, and sewer grates. They saw people pushing shopping carts filled with all their belongings. The painful reality was that across the United States more than 735,000 people were homeless, surviving on the streets or in shelters.

What caused homelessness in America? Several things:

• *Cuts in the federal public housing program.* In 1976, the government built 167,000 units of low-rent housing. In 1989, it built only 25,000. And the waiting list for public housing was growing longer.

• *Higher rents.* In the 1950s, people spent about 20 percent of their income on rent. By 1985, the figure for low-income families ranged from 50 percent to 70 percent.

• *Urban renewal.* During the 1980s, many large cities carried out urban renewal programs in which they put up modern apartment buildings. These buildings replaced hotels and boardinghouses where poor, usually single people used to rent rooms. With their cheap lodgings gone, these people could not afford a place to live.

• *Release of the mentally ill from institutions.* During the 1970s, states and cities adopted a new policy. They decided that many mentally ill people would be better off in the community than in a mental hospital. So the states and cities released many patients who, it turned out, were not ready to function in the community. These people made up part of the homeless population.

Many churches and private groups opened shelters for the homeless during the 1980s. But the fact remained: homelessness was a modern-day American tragedy.

A Changing Court

The U.S. Supreme Court building, Washington, D.C.

In the 1980s, most Americans had strong opinions about the Supreme Court. The Court's opinions became more conservative then, and Americans disagreed sharply about whether this was good or bad.

From the mid-1950s through the 1970s, the Court made many decisions about people's rights. Among other things, it ruled against school segregation (1954), it increased the rights of people accused of crimes (1963 and 1966), and it legalized abortion (1973).

Many Americans supported these decisions. By the early 1970s, however, a number of Americans felt that the Court was going too far. They felt the Court was getting too powerful—that it was making up new laws instead of deciding what the existing laws meant.

The Republican party agreed. Its candidates for the presidency promised to appoint conservative judges to the Supreme Court. They wanted judges who believed that the federal government should play a limited role in people's lives and that the courts should protect only those rights already clearly guaranteed by law. The Republicans won every presidential election between 1968 and 1988 except the one in 1976. As a result of Republican presidential appointments, by the 1990s, most of the Court's nine justices were conservative. Many experts believe the Supreme Court will remain conservative for years to come.

What kind of decisions is a conservative Supreme Court likely to hand down? We can get some idea by looking at some decisions the Court recently made in the areas of affirmative action, job discrimination, and abortion.

U. of California Regents v. Bakke

Allan Bakke, a white man in his 30s, wanted to become a doctor. He applied to the medical school at the University of California but was turned down twice. Then he learned that the school admitted students based on a quota.

A *quota* is a fixed number of openings that a company or school reserves for minority groups. In the past, women and minorities were denied education and jobs because of their sex and race. Many people wanted to right these wrongs. In the 1960s and 1970s, Supreme Court rulings called for *affirmative action*, a plan to help people overcome discrimination. Supporters believed that guaranteeing places for women and minorities would help them succeed and overcome discrimination. So the University of California Medical School set aside 16 out of 100 openings for African-Americans, Hispanics, and Asians.

Bakke sued the university. He charged that he was a victim of reverse discrimination. He felt he was being discriminated against because he was white. He pointed out that some of the 16 minority students who were admitted had grade point averages that were lower than his. This violated the U.S. Constitution, he said. The 14th Amendment guarantees that everyone is entitled to "the equal protection of the laws."

The Supreme Court made two decisions. On one hand, it ruled that racial quotas violate the Civil Rights Act of 1964. Therefore, Bakke had to be admitted to the medical school. On the

Allan Bakke, whose case led to a Supreme Court ruling against racial quotas.

other hand, said the Court, race may be taken into consideration in school admissions to right past wrongs. But it can't be the *only* consideration.

Wards Cove Packing Company Inc. v. Atonio

In 1989, the Supreme Court made another important decision that showed its conservative views. Frank Atonio and nine nonwhite co-workers sued their company for discrimination. They said that the Wards Cove Packing Company hired whites for the best jobs and that the unskilled, lowest-paying jobs went to nonwhites like themselves, who rarely got promoted.

The company's own statistics seemed to support these complaints. Whites did hold most of the good jobs. But the Supreme Court ruled that numbers alone don't prove discrimination. This was a change from many of its earlier decisions. The Court also shifted the burden of proof from the company to the worker. Before, a company had to prove that it did *not* discriminate. Now, a worker had to prove that the company *did* discriminate.

Clarence Thomas, a conservative (top), became a Supreme Court Justice in 1991. He was opposed by liberals and was accused of sexual harassment. After televised hearings, the Senate approved Thomas by a close vote. Below, the Court in 1990.

Webster v. Reproductive Health Services

The new Supreme Court also took a conservative stand on abortion. Before 1973, some states allowed abortions, while others did not. In 1973, in *Roe v. Wade*, the Supreme Court declared that abortions were legal everywhere in the country. Since then, people who opposed this decision have been trying to make abortion illegal.

In 1986, the state of Missouri passed a law that sharply restricted abortions. Under this law, tax-supported hospitals and public employees could not perform abortions except to save the mother's life.

In 1989, in *Webster v. Reproductive Health Services*, the Supreme Court upheld the Missouri law. Chief Justice William Rehnquist said, "Nothing in the Constitution requires states to enter or remain in the business of performing abortions." So the Court saw no reason to overturn the Missouri law. The decision made it clear that a majority of the Court did not consider abortion to be within our constitutional rights.

Rust v. Sullivan

The Court also showed a conservative view of abortion in *Rust v. Sullivan*, a 1991 decision. In 1970, the federal government had begun funding about 4,000 public health clinics that cared for 4 million low-income women each year. In 1988, the Reagan administration issued new guidelines for these clinics. It said that doctors in federally-funded clinics could no longer counsel patients about abortion – not even if the patients asked

A Woman on the Court

During his 1980 presidential campaign, Ronald Reagan promised to appoint a woman to the Supreme Court. In 1981, when Justice Potter Stewart retired, Reagan appointed Sandra Day O'Connor. She is the first woman to serve on the nation's highest court.

O'Connor graduated from the Stanford University law school in California. She worked as a lawyer, was an Arizona state senator, and then became a judge. So far, Justice O'Connor has usually voted on the side of conservatives. But she has a mind of her own. Reported *The Atlantic* magazine, O'Connor ". . . appears to keep one eye on the Constitution, one eye on the real world, and an open mind to judge what she sees."

questions about
the procedure. Only if
a woman's life was in danger would
abortion counseling be allowed.

Dr. Irving Rust, who worked in a
New York clinic, objected. He said that
the rules would force him to commit
malpractice – to practice medicine
improperly. "This case is about
suppressing information between a
patient and her doctor," he said. "The
Government has interfered in that
relationship." Rust sued the
government. In May of 1991, the
Supreme Court ruled in favor of the
government.

Many people disagreed with the
ruling. They felt it discriminated
against poor women. Rich women,
they said, could get whatever medical
information they needed. Poor women
could not. Many critics also argued that
the decision violated the right to free
speech.

Supporters of the decision argued
that U.S. taxpayers should not have to
pay for a practice that many people felt
was immoral.

Overall, Americans were
divided about the conservative
Supreme Court. Some said that the
Court was correcting the excesses of
the liberal Court of the 1960s and
1970s. Others said that it was undoing
many good decisions. ∎

*Quotas have been a big issue in recent
presidential elections. What do you think
of quotas? Do you think they are fair?
Why or why not?*

*Arguments over abortion are very heated
throughout the United States. Activists on
both sides of the issue hold rallies and
demonstrations. Antiabortion activists
often block entrances to abortion clinics.
How do you feel about these tactics? Do
you think they are effective? Give reasons
to support your opinion.*

**Antiabortion
protesters
demonstrating in
Wichita, Kansas,
in 1991.**

CRIME IN THE STREETS

The United States has always had crime. But in the 1980s, it seemed to be getting worse. In 1989, crime touched one in every four households in America. In the inner cities, it touched nearly one in three. Many Americans think that crime is this country's most serious problem – and that it will only get worse.

Causes of the Crime Wave

Why is there so much crime in the United States? People have suggested many different reasons. Poverty and drugs are the two most often mentioned. Poverty increased during the 1980s. Also, the Reagan administration reduced money for many federal programs that helped poor Americans. As a result, some think that many poor people turned to crime out of desperation.

Drugs have also been blamed for the rise in crime. Between 1985 and 1989, the number of drug arrests increased from 800,000 to more than 1.3 million. Users often become "hooked" on drugs and spend all their money buying them. Many drug addicts turn to crime to support their habit.

Gang-related crimes have also increased, largely due to drugs. In the 1980s, crack – an inexpensive form of cocaine – hit the streets. Gangs made large amounts of money selling the drug. Many neighborhoods became war zones, as rival gangs fought to control the drug trade.

The increase in crime has filled America's prisons. The U.S. prison population increased by over 100 percent between 1980 and 1989. Already over 1 million by 1990, the prison population showed no sign of

Gang graffiti spray-painted on an inner city building. Gangs turned many neighborhoods into war zones.

By 1990, America's prison population was over 1 million.

shrinking. The government can't build new prisons fast enough to keep up with all the new prisoners. And this, some believe, has helped worsen the crime problem: they feel that criminals can "slip through the cracks" of an overburdened justice system.

Locking 'Em Up

In May of 1989, President Bush unveiled a new anticrime program. Among other things, he said he wanted to spend $1 billion to build new federal prisons.

Would society benefit from spending so much money? Many experts don't think so. Studies show that putting people in prison does little to reduce crime. In fact, some experts believe that many convicts who are released after a few years are likely to commit more crimes. Of one group of prisoners released in 1983, nearly half were convicted of another crime within three years.

What *might* work? Many new ideas are being suggested. Some private companies are offering to manage prisons. They say they could do the job better and more cheaply than the government. By 1988, one company had contracts from five states to run 11 different prisons.

Other prison reformers are calling for a program called "smart punishment." This plan uses a combination of prison time and outside supervision. For example, a criminal might have to spend 90 days in a military-style "boot camp," work for a community service program, and pay the victim of the crime for damages.

A federal officer displaying some of the illegal weapons seized by Boston police in 1990.

Judges in Phoenix, Arizona, now have 22 nonprison options to choose from.

These and other new ideas are not yet widely used. But as the prison populations continue to rise, many Americans are willing to try new solutions. ■

Do you agree or disagree that crime is this country's most serious problem—and that it will only get worse? Write a few paragraphs about your point of view. Use personal experiences to support your opinion.

What do you think of the ideas mentioned to reform the prison system—private management of prisons and "smart punishment"? Do you have any other ideas for prison reform?

Gun Control: Yes or No

According to a 1988 poll, nearly half of all Americans own at least one gun. Yet nearly 80 percent of Americans polled that same year wanted stricter laws covering gun sales.

In 1981, John Hinckley tried to kill President Ronald Reagan with a handgun. Reagan's press secretary, James Brady, was caught in the cross fire and disabled for life. In 1991, Congress approved the so-called Brady Bill. The bill requires a seven-day waiting period for anyone buying a handgun. During the waiting period, police can check the buyer's background. The gun dealer must refuse to sell to anyone with a criminal record or a history of drug abuse or mental illness.

For Gun Control

Supporters of the Brady Bill argued that it was a step toward keeping handguns out of the hands of dangerous criminals. Democratic representative Edward F. Feighan of Ohio said that "Since the last time we considered the Brady Bill, in 1988, 50,000 Americans have died as a result of handgun violence." Dewey Stokes, president of the Fraternal Order of Police, agreed. "No one claims gun control will stop all gun-related crime.

But a survey found that 28 percent of prison inmates said they had bought firearms over the counter. Stopping 28 percent of crime would be significant."

Against Gun Control

The National Rifle Association opposed the Brady Bill. This group felt that the bill interfered with people's right to defend themselves against criminals. Wayne LaPierre, explaining the NRA position, also argued that waiting periods "don't cut crime. Honest people would face bureaucratic nightmares while criminals operated outside the system."

The War on Drugs

Not long after American troops pulled out of the Vietnam War in 1973, Americans found themselves fighting a different kind of war at home. The enemy this time was illegal drugs. By the 1980s, one of these drugs – cocaine – had become a bigger problem than all the rest. Cocaine began as a plaything of the rich, who often sniffed it at parties. Then, in the mid-1980s, "crack" cocaine – which is smoked rather than sniffed – appeared. Soon, it became the drug of choice for those who couldn't afford cocaine.

Money and the Cocaine Boom

Cocaine is made from the leaves of the coca plant, which grows in South America. Bolivia, Colombia, and Peru started growing large amounts of coca in the 1980s – because that seemed to be the only way their starving farmers could earn a living.

Cocaine production is a *very* profitable business. It is estimated that Americans spend $110 billion on drugs each year. That's more than twice the profits of the nation's 500 largest corporations – combined. And because drugs are illegal, the profits from drug sales are tax-free.

Fighting a Losing Battle

President Ronald Reagan tried to use the armed forces to keep cocaine out of the United States. He used troops to patrol the nation's borders to prevent drug smuggling. It didn't work. In 1987, for example, the air force spent $2.6 million and made only 10 drug arrests. The navy spent $40 million and seized only 20 packages of drugs. As

The U.S. Coast Guard (top) seizing drugs being smuggled into the country. Bolivian farmers (bottom) selling coca leaves, the source of cocaine, at a street-corner market in Bolivia.

critics of this approach point out, the United States has a 2,000-mile border with Mexico, a 3,000-mile border with Canada, and thousands of miles of shoreline. That makes it almost impossible to prevent drug smuggling.

The United States also tried to convince South American countries to grow other crops such as coffee. But since other crops don't bring in the money that cocaine does, that approach hasn't worked either. In 1986, U.S. troops went into Bolivia. They destroyed cocaine-producing laboratories and helped catch some drug producers. But cocaine-producing operations just moved elsewhere.

President George Bush continued to use troops in the drug war. His administration focused on controlling the production and sale of illegal drugs.

A Bolivian police officer guarding a cocaine factory after a police raid.

Crack Children

They can be uncontrollably wild. They're easily upset. Many are disturbed by sounds; others panic when touched. Because they have trouble playing with other children, they withdraw into themselves. They can't concentrate for long, so they learn language slowly. They have trouble learning colors and shapes and even with learning their own names.

They are "crack babies," the children of women who smoked crack while pregnant. These damaged children are a national tragedy. And caring for them is quickly becoming a major problem. A 1991 study showed that about 10 percent of all newborns – 375,000 babies a

year – are exposed to drugs before they are born. Cocaine – including crack – is the drug most addicted mothers use.

Some believe that with good care and education, crack children can grow up normally. Others aren't so hopeful. "I don't imagine that he'll ever be like other kids," says one mother about her four-year-old.

Some people predict that within a few years up to 60 percent of American school-aged kids will have been exposed to drugs in the womb. For these children who begin their lives at such a disadvantage, the future does not look bright. And no one knows for sure what problems they will face as adults.

Other Ways of Fighting Drugs

Other Americans have tried to win the drug war by decreasing the demand for drugs. For example, First Lady Nancy Reagan began a public campaign. She and other famous people encouraged young people to "just say no" to drugs.

Other Americans think we should legalize drug use. They believe that this would take the profit out of drug dealing and reduce crime. It would also help the nation's criminal justice system, which is now overloaded with drug arrests. The United States could even tax the sale of drugs and use the money for antidrug education. Most Americans, though, disagree. They believe that legalizing drugs would only cause more people to use them than before.

Some Americans think more drug treatment centers are the answer. Because of the shortage of centers, barely one out of 10 people needing treatment can get it. Very few treatment programs will treat pregnant addicts, a growing part of the cocaine-using crowd.

Some Americans feel it would be smarter to concentrate on improving the nation's economy. They point out that in the late 1980s, drug abuse among the upper and middle classes dropped, while it increased among the poor. If fewer people were poor, they argue, fewer would use drugs. Others point out that many drug users are not poor; in fact, two-thirds of all drug users have jobs. Some are very wealthy.

There seem to be no easy answers to the drug problem. ■

THEN & NOW

Drug use among America's young people peaked in 1982. That year, 64.4 percent of high school seniors said they had used an illegal drug. Ever since the 1960s, when drugs started becoming popular, more and more young people had been trying them.

In recent years, though, drug use has been declining among young people. By 1989, the National Institute on Drug Abuse reported that only 50.9 percent of high school seniors had used an illegal drug. Says Ted Sanders, the under secretary of education, "No one can be completely satisfied with a report that tells us more than half of our young people try at least one illegal drug before graduating from high school." But he adds that the survey shows that perhaps "we can again become a society where drug abuse is a rare exception rather than an expected behavior among our youth."

Several rap groups perform songs with the "just say no" theme. Get together with one or two others. Write a brief rap song about your opinion of drug use.

People marching (below) to make others aware of the drug problem.

The Greedy 1980s

"Greed is all right, by the way," the graduation speaker told the class of 1985. "I think greed is healthy. You can be greedy and still feel good about yourself."

Graduating college seniors laughed and applauded this speech by Ivan Boesky. Twenty years earlier, they would have booed him off the stage. But times—and values—change. In many ways, Boesky—one of several Wall Street deal makers who ended up in prison for being greedy and dishonest—was the voice of the 1980s.

That voice was echoed in the movie *Wall Street*. This 1987 film showed how easily the lure of easy money can corrupt people. It was the urge to get rich quick that caused white-collar crime to soar in the 1980s. (A "white-collar" worker does not do physical labor but works in an office.) Stealing

Businessmen walking down New York City's famous Wall Street, the "financial capital of the world."

company money and not paying taxes are examples of white-collar crime.

Wall Street's Miracle Man

Ivan Boesky made a fortune on the stock market. He did it by buying the stocks of companies that he believed would be bought by other companies. After a company is taken over by another company, the price of its stock usually rises. People who buy that stock before the takeover and sell it afterward can make a large profit.

Boesky guessed right much of the time. But he lost about $70 million in 1984, when a takeover bid he was counting on failed to occur. Reeling from that loss, Boesky decided to cheat. He started buying inside information about upcoming deals from an investment banker.

Both Boesky and the banker, Dennis Levine, made millions in 1985. But the Securities and Exchange Commission (SEC), a government agency, was tipped off to Levine's activities. The SEC watches over stock and bond dealers to make sure they're being honest with investors.

In mid-1986, SEC officials arrested Dennis Levine for insider trading, which is against the law. Levine quickly informed on other cheaters. That led the SEC to Boesky, who identified even more cheaters. The one who most interested the government was Michael Milken.

Inventor of the Junk Bond

Michael Milken was the king of the "junk bond" market that made most of the decade's mergers and takeovers possible. A junk bond is a bond that is considered a risky investment. As a result, it sells for a low price but offers higher interest than costlier top-grade bonds. Milken convinced people that they could make more money by investing in "junk."

Both Ivan Boesky (left) and Michael Milken (right) made millions of dollars illegally.

He was right. Companies made quick profits on junk bonds. Then they used those profits to buy other companies. And each time they did, they paid Milken a fee. Milken's junk-bond department at Drexel Burnham Lambert turned the company into Wall Street's most powerful investment firm. Other investment firms, too, created junk-bond departments.

Drexel paid its star employee extremely well. In one year alone, Milken made more than $500 million. But Milken wanted more – more excitement. He liked living on the edge. He spared little time for sleeping or eating. He was up nearly 20 hours a day, making bigger and better deals. Some of the deals weren't legal.

The government spent four years preparing its case against Milken. It accused him of insider trading, bribery, cheating on taxes, fixing stock prices, and much more. In 1989, Milken paid $600 million in fines and penalties. Late in 1990, a judge sentenced Milken to 10 years in prison. By the middle of 1991, Drexel Burnham Lambert was bankrupt. ■

Beyond the Moon

The last crew of the space shuttle *Challenger*. All seven died when the shuttle exploded in flight. Christa McAuliffe (second row, second from left) was the first citizen passenger on a space flight.

Since our space program began in 1958, the United States has had an exciting list of accomplishments: satellites in space, humans orbiting the earth, even people landing and walking on the moon. But what would the space program do next? The National Aeronautics and Space Administration (NASA) decided to send people into space to fix satellites and to do medical experiments. NASA wanted to send them on a special, new kind of space vehicle—one that could be used again and again. It named the new program the Space Transportation System. For short, NASA called it the space shuttle.

A Reusable Spaceship

Unlike earlier spaceships, much of the shuttle was designed to be reused. The orbiter, in which the crew lives and works, would fly back to Earth and land like an airplane. The two solid rocket boosters (SRBs) that help lift the shuttle into orbit would fall into the ocean. There, they would be picked up and used again.

By building such a space shuttle, NASA hoped to make space travel "less costly and more routine." Eventually, the shuttle might operate like a small lab for science experiments. It could also be used for space research by the military, teachers, or businesspeople.

Disaster and Success

"Obviously a major malfunction. . . . We have a report from the Flight Dynamics Officer that the vehicle has exploded." These words from NASA Mission Control spokesman Steve Nesbitt only confirmed what millions of shocked Americans had seen for themselves on TV. On January 28, 1986, at 11:39 A.M., the space shuttle *Challenger* had exploded high in the Florida sky. All seven crew members, including high school teacher Christa McAuliffe, were dead.

President Reagan appointed a group of scientists to find why the *Challenger* exploded. Their report states, "The cause of the accident was a failure of the (O-ring) pressure seal . . . of the right solid rocket motor." But the experts could not decide what had weakened the seal. Cold launch-day temperatures, sand or water getting through the seal, and the design of the rocket itself all may have helped cause the explosion.

After the *Challenger* accident, NASA created a safety panel. The panel's job was to check the design of new rockets and vehicles to prevent another accident. NASA also changed the way the shuttle program was managed. After 2½ years of work, NASA succeeded. The shuttle *Discovery* lifted off on September 29, 1988. The United States was back in space. ■

Christa McAuliffe

On August 27, 1984, President Reagan announced he wanted the first citizen passenger on the space shuttle to be "one of America's finest: a teacher." Christa McAuliffe heard the president. Her husband told her, "Go for it."

From thousands of teachers who applied, Christa McAuliffe was picked to ride the shuttle. Once the shuttle reached orbit, McAuliffe planned to teach lessons that would be televised to schools throughout the country. Students across the nation looked forward to the first "outer space" classroom.

Christa McAuliffe's dream of teaching from space would have made the *Challenger* flight something special for everyone.

High school teacher Christa McAuliffe was the first citizen passenger to fly on a U.S. space mission. Do you think civilians should take part in future space shuttle flights?

Would you want to go into space? If so, what kind of mission would you choose? If not, what are your reasons?

Challenger exploding, January 28, 1986.

THE SHUTTLE EXPLODES

6 IN CREW AND HIGH-SCHOOL TEACHER ARE KILLED 74 SECONDS AFTER LIFTOFF

SDAY, JANUARY 29, 1986

Thousands Watch
A Rain of Debris

By WILLIAM J. BROAD

CAPE CANAVERAL, Fla., Jan. 28 — The space shuttle Challenger exploded in a ball of fire shortly after it left the launching pad today, and all seven astronauts on board were lost.

The worst accident in the history of the American space program, it was witnessed by thousands

PERSONAL COMPUTERS

The personal computer revolution had a humble beginning. In 1975, two young men built the first easy-to-use computer in a garage. Within three years, their new company, Apple Computers, was leading a revolution in computer use.

The personal computer, or PC, was remarkable. It was small enough to fit on top of a desk. It could store large amounts of information. It was cheap; small businesses and even individuals could afford one.

Special computer programs, called *software*, helped people write and calculate easily on the new machines. PC sales skyrocketed. As the number of computers grew, so did the amount of software, making computers more useful. Special software for manufacturing, medicine, law, accounting, and even art and music made the PC a powerful tool. Teachers began to use the PC to teach reading, math, spelling, and writing skills.

Today, computer companies create new generations of their computers. Each new batch has two or three times the speed and storage ability of the earlier generation. And with each new generation comes better and more powerful software. As a result, many artists using the computers and software can create better images – even animation. Businesses can manage their money more efficiently and improve sales. Doctors can make faster, more accurate diagnoses. Thanks to the personal computer, America is firmly entrenched in the computer age. ■

Pac-Man (top), a cartoon figure in one of the first popular computer video games. The Apple Macintosh (bottom), one of the personal computers introduced during the 1980s.

THEN & NOW

Just days after Nolan Bushnell placed his new coin-operated video game, Pong, in a California bar, it broke down. When Bushnell came to repair the machine, he found what was wrong: the machine was so popular it was stuffed to overflowing with quarters!

In the 20 years since Pong was introduced, the popularity of electronic games has exploded. Companies have made millions of dollars creating games such as Pong, Space Invaders, Pac-Man, and Mario Brothers. Many of the games have become household names around the world. As one writer put it, "electronic entertainment has become a global fact of life."

Three Mile Island

Holly Garnish lived a quarter of a mile from the Three Mile Island (TMI) nuclear power plant in Pennsylvania. At four o'clock in the morning on March 28, 1979, she heard a loud noise from the plant. "Picture the biggest jet at an airport and the sound it makes. That's what I heard. It shook the windows, the whole house," Garnish told writer Mark Stephens.

The noise was a blast of steam from a safety valve on the TMI Unit 2 (TMI-2) building, which housed a nuclear reactor for generating electricity. The steam was radioactive, and it signaled the start of the worst nuclear accident the nation had known.

Because of equipment problems and human errors, the TMI-2 reactor had lost much of the water that cooled the hot solid fuel at its core. As heat and radiation built up inside the reactor, workers struggled to understand what was happening. Precious time was lost. The reactor was badly damaged.

Meltdown!

People worried that the reactor's core would melt because of the extreme heat. They feared that the solid fuel would break through its container or explode, spreading deadly

The Three Mile Island nuclear power plant, the site of a major nuclear accident in 1979.

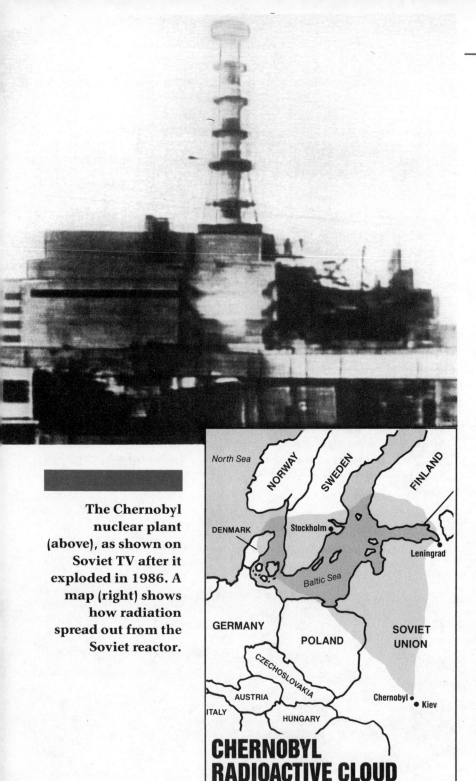

melted. Frank Standerfer, TMI-2 director, said after seeing the core damage, "We're surprised the reactor vessel contained the accident." But it did; the steel container that held the core helped prevent a massive release of radioactivity in Pennsylvania.

Explosion at Chernobyl

The people of Chernobyl in the Soviet Union were not so lucky. In April of 1986, a different type of nuclear reactor *did* explode. It sent a huge cloud of radioactive matter high into the air. Winds carried the poisonous cloud hundreds of miles across the Soviet Union and Europe. Rain carried the radioactivity to earth.

The explosion killed many people immediately. Others died slowly from diseases caused by radioactivity. As late as 1991, many areas near Chernobyl were so radioactive that people still could not live in them.

The Three Mile Island and Chernobyl accidents convinced some people that the dangers of nuclear power were far greater than the benefits. They pointed to the 10 years and nearly $1 billion required to clean up TMI-2. They remembered the lost lives and poisoned environment from Chernobyl. But with energy supplies threatened by war and the environment polluted by oil spills, the nuclear power debate is far from over. To many, nuclear power still is an attractive form of energy. ■

Do you worry about the danger of a nuclear meltdown at a plant like Three Mile Island? Would you be concerned about living near such a plant? Answer these questions for yourself, and then ask them of 10 people you know. Write a paragraph summarizing the results of your poll.

The Chernobyl nuclear plant (above), as shown on Soviet TV after it exploded in 1986. A map (right) shows how radiation spread out from the Soviet reactor.

North Sea
NORWAY
SWEDEN
FINLAND
DENMARK
Stockholm
Leningrad
Baltic Sea
GERMANY
POLAND
SOVIET UNION
CZECHOSLOVAKIA
AUSTRIA
ITALY
HUNGARY
Chernobyl • Kiev

CHERNOBYL RADIOACTIVE CLOUD

radioactivity. Because there was no explosion or damage to the container, experts on the scene *thought* there had not been a meltdown. But years later, as they finished cleaning up TMI-2, engineers realized that the damage was much worse than they had believed. At least 70 percent of the core was damaged. And even more startling, 35 to 45 percent of the core had actually

A New Disease to Conquer

The young doctor was worried. Within a short time, he had seen two patients with the same unusual symptoms. And their immune systems, the body's means of fighting infection, were not working. The same problems began showing up in more patients. The doctor, Michael Gottlieb, said, "I realized then that this was something far bigger than anyone might have suspected."

Gottlieb wrote about his experiences and sent the information to the U.S. Centers for Disease Control (CDC). On June 5, 1981, Gottlieb's findings were published. For the first time, the world became aware of acquired immune deficiency syndrome, or AIDS.

"Nothing Like This Before"

"There simply has never been anything quite like this before," said Jonathan Mann, director of the World Health Organization's (WHO) Global Program on AIDS. The disease is caused by a virus called the *human immunodeficiency virus* (HIV). The virus lives in human body fluids, such as semen and blood. It can be spread through sexual contact, sharing of needles to use intravenous drugs, and blood transfusions. Pregnant women with the HIV virus can also pass on the disease to their children.

The HIV virus can live in a person's body for months—even for years—before it develops into AIDS. Once a person has AIDS, the body's immune system gradually breaks down. The body can no longer fight infections that a healthy system could easily fight off. People with AIDS often die from rare forms of pneumonia or cancer.

In the first 10 years after Gottlieb's discovery, nearly 100,000 Americans died from AIDS. Another quarter of a million died from the disease around the world. The World Health Organization believes that by 1991, 8 to 10 million people worldwide were already HIV-infected. Some experts think this number could increase to 20 million by the year 2000. In Africa, AIDS is the number-one public health problem. Twenty to 40 percent of the people in some African cities carry the HIV virus.

When AIDS was first discovered, homosexual men in the United States made up the majority of known AIDS victims. Some people thought of AIDS as a disease of gay men. But Dr. Gottlieb reminds people, "It's important to get across that AIDS is not

Basketball superstar Earvin "Magic" Johnson announcing his retirement after testing positive for the HIV virus.

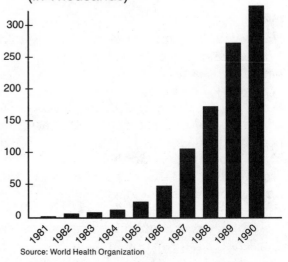

AIDS CASES
Number of Reported
Cases Worldwide, 1981-1990
(in Thousands)

Source: World Health Organization

Members of ACT-UP at the California state capitol, protesting budget cuts for health services.

a gay disease. . . ." Risky behavior— such as not using condoms, not knowing the background of sexual partners, or sharing dirty needles for IV drugs—puts anyone in danger of getting AIDS.

Although AIDS is caused by a virus, it may be possible to develop a vaccine to prevent the disease. Doctors are working on a vaccine that may help people already infected. But effective treatments and cures are years away. In spite of billions of dollars spent on research, this deadly new disease still kills. ■

As a public service, TV and billboard ads warn the public about the danger of AIDS. These ads sometimes use graphic or blunt language about sex and drugs that offends people. Do you think this kind of information should be presented in this way? Why or why not?

The AIDS Memorial Quilt and ACT-UP

People have responded to the AIDS tragedy in very different ways. Some prefer to quietly remember those who have died. Others become stirred to act or to express anger at their loss.

The Memorial Quilt started in San Francisco in 1987. People who had lost loved ones to AIDS began to sew quilt squares that showed something about the victim's life. Within months, the idea had spread around the country. By 1988, the Names Project had assembled more than 8,000 squares into a 16-ton quilt the size of eight football fields. The quilt

eventually traveled to 20 cities throughout the United States.

The gay activist group ACT-UP (AIDS Coalition To Unleash Power) has responded differently to the AIDS tragedy. It works to speed development of drugs and treatments for AIDS victims. It also protests and lobbies for more government involvement in the fight against AIDS. Some argue that ACT-UP doesn't focus on the best weapon against AIDS— prevention. But ACT-UP members say they are fighting for people for whom prevention is too late— people who already have AIDS.

Oil on the Water

The driver simply missed a turn. Usually, that's not a big problem. But when the driver is steering a 987-foot-long supertanker carrying millions of gallons of oil, missing a turn can lead to disaster.

The supertanker *Exxon Valdez* had just left the Alaskan port of Valdez. It was filled with crude oil. Shortly after midnight on March 24, 1989, an inexperienced third mate was piloting the ship. He was not certified to pilot the tanker in those iceberg-studded waters. The *Exxon Valdez* crashed into the jagged rocks of Bligh Reef. Before long, more than 10 million gallons of oil had leaked into the clear waters of Prince William Sound. It was the largest oil spill in U.S. history.

The oil slick soon covered more than 1,000 miles of shoreline. Beaches became coated with sticky black oil. Seabirds, sea otters, bald eagles, and other wildlife died by the thousands. The fishing industry in the sound was nearly destroyed.

Workers (above) cleaning up the Alaskan shore after the damaged *Exxon Valdez* (below) leaked more than 10 million gallons of oil into the ocean.

The Exxon Corporation spent $1 billion to clean up Prince William Sound. It used water sprays to clean up the beaches and special bacteria to eat the oil. More than 11,000 people helped to clean up the spill. The long-term damage to the environment of the sound will be great. And many of the disaster's other effects may take years to show up.

The map shows the area covered by the *Exxon Valdez* oil slick. The oil drifted 300 miles south from the accident.

The Big Spill

Only nine months later, on the other side of the world, there was an explosion on the Iranian supertanker *Khark 5,* off the coast of Morocco. This time, 19 million gallons of oil – nearly twice the amount of the Alaskan spill – created a 217-mile-long slick in the Atlantic Ocean. Although the Alaskan cleanup was criticized for being too slow, the *Khark 5* cleanup was worse. It did not even begin for almost two weeks. Jacques Cousteau, the French ocean expert, said, "It's just unbelievable. A major disaster, and nobody moves." Fortunately, the *Khark 5* slick stayed far out to sea and broke up without causing major environmental damage. ■

The Exxon Valdez *accident was a big topic of conversation in the United States in 1989–1990. Many people blamed the boat's captain or the Exxon Corporation for failing to protect the environment. What do you think? Should exploring for oil be controlled more by the government? Should certain places* not *be explored – even if this drives up the price of oil?*

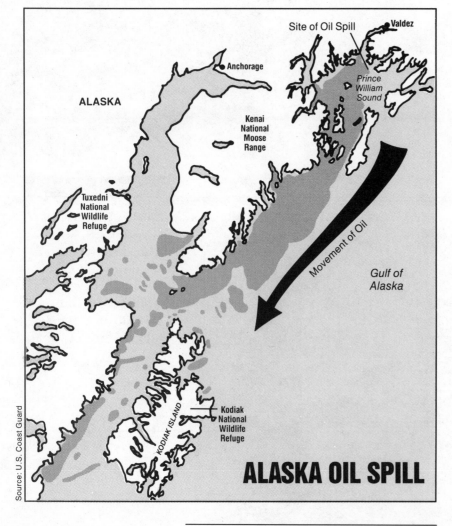

Source: U.S. Coast Guard

Site of Oil Spill — Valdez

Anchorage

ALASKA

Kenai National Moose Range

Prince William Sound

Tuxedni National Wildlife Refuge

Movement of Oil

Gulf of Alaska

KODIAK ISLAND

Kodiak National Wildlife Refuge

ALASKA OIL SPILL

Oil Spills: The Search for Answers

The *Exxon Valdez* and *Khark 5* oil disasters made people in the United States ask some important questions. Should oil exploration be allowed near the Arctic National Wildlife Refuge? What kinds of environmental changes could such exploration and drilling cause? Should supertankers be built with double hulls to protect against damage and spills? Could spill cleanup be improved and sped up to reduce damage to the environment? As America depends more on imported oil, the search for answers to these questions becomes more urgent.

* This symbol before a page number indicates a photograph of the subject mentioned.

Credits

Photo Credits

AP/Wide World Photos: 50b
Courtesy Apple Computers: 3b, 86
Neil Benson: 34
The Bettmann Archives: 6b, 11b, 13a, 20b, 21b, 29, 30, 31a, 50a, 51ab, 54, 61b, 64, 66, 69b, 73, 79a, 80, 81, 83ab, 87, 91b
Courtesy Cherokee Nation: 27
Courtesy Chicago Bulls: 3a, 53
Foundation for Advancements in Science and Education. Tony Friedkin Photo, © 1991: 28
Craig T. Kojima, Honolulu Star-Bulletin: 68
Dennis MacDonald: 77
Darren Michaels: 43
Courtesy Nabisco Brands, Inc.: 63
Courtesy NASA: 84, 85
Roger Neal: 33
Courtesy New York Convention and Visitors Bureau: 82
Pac-MAN™ and © 1980 NAMCO Ltd. All rights reserved: 86
Courtesy Office of The City Representative, City of Philadelphia: 6a
Photofest: 38, 39, 40, 41, 42
Steve Rasmussen: 75
Root Studios: 47
Andy Schwartz/Photofest: 37
Courtesy Kristi Simkins: 76
Courtesy Ian Steer: 58
Collection of the Supreme Court of the U.S.: 72
Courtesy Supreme Court Historical Society: 74b
Randall Thomas, The Salvation Army: 70
United Press International: 2a, 12a, 13b, 14, 15, 16, 17, 18, 19, 20a, 22ab, 24abcd, 25, 26, 31b, 35, 49a, 52ab, 55, 56a, 57ab, 60ab, 61a, 65, 71, 74a, 78, 88, 89, 90, 91a
Courtesy USTA/Russ Adams: 56b
Courtesy U.S. Coast Guard Photography: 79b
David Valdez, The White House: 69a